THE HIGHER CIVIL SERVICE

The Higher Civil Service

An Evaluation of Federal Personnel Practices

DAVID T. STANLEY

THE BROOKINGS INSTITUTION • *Washington, D. C.*

© 1964 by

THE BROOKINGS INSTITUTION

Published November 1964

Second Printing June 1971

Library of Congress Catalogue Card Number 64-66213

ISBN 0-8157-8104-0

THE BROOKINGS INSTITUTION is an independent organization devoted to nonpartisan research, education, and publication in economics, government, foreign policy, and the social sciences generally. Its principal purposes are to aid in the development of sound public policies and to promote public understanding of issues of national importance.

The Institution was founded December 8, 1927, to merge the activities of the Institute for Government Research, founded in 1916, the Institute of Economics, founded in 1922, and the Robert Brookings Graduate School of Economics and Government, founded in 1924.

The general administration of the Institution is the responsibility of a self-perpetuating Board of Trustees. The Trustees are likewise charged with maintaining the independence of the staff and fostering the most favorable conditions for creative research and education. The immediate direction of the policies, program, and staff of the Institution is vested in the President, assisted by the division directors and an advisory council, chosen from the professional staff of the Institution.

In publishing a study, the Institution presents it as a competent treatment of a subject worthy of public consideration. The interpretations and conclusions in such publications are those of the author or authors and do not purport to represent the views of the other staff members, officers, or trustees of the Brookings Institution.

Foreword

THIS BRIEF STUDY of the higher federal civil service grew out of letters and discussions between the United States Civil Service Commission and the Governmental Studies staff of the Brookings Institution. Originally proposed as an evaluation of "rank-in-job" versus "rank-in-man" principles, it broadened into a study of policies, procedures, and institutional concepts affecting higher federal personnel. It is intended to be a realistic assessment of the federal government's use of higher scientific, professional, and managerial employees. Positive and negative elements in the present situation are discussed and alternative arrangements evaluated.

The study was directed by David T. Stanley of the Senior Staff under the general supervision of George A. Graham, Director of Governmental Studies. Miss Frances M. Shattuck was the principal research assistant. Interviewing was done for Brookings by Rowland E. Dietz, Laurin L. Henry, and Waldo Sommers. Mrs. Frances C. Mills served as both interviewer and research assistant. The following served as interviewers on assignment from federal agencies: Richard W. Bunch, Department of Health, Education, and Welfare; Thomas W. Carr, Civil Service Commission; Dillon S. Myer, Agency for International Development; [1] and Peter Storm, Bureau of the Budget. The manuscript was edited by Adele Garrett. Miss Deborah Bliss was responsible for secretarial and administrative work, with the aid of Miss E. Rebecca Roper. Valuable records search work was contributed by the staff of the Federal Records Center, St. Louis, under M. D. Davies, Chief, Reference Service Branch. Coding and tabulating services were supplied by National Analysts, Inc., of Philadelphia.

The project director had the counsel of an advisory committee consisting of Marver H. Bernstein of Princeton University, Joseph Charyk

[1] Mr. Myer also served briefly as a Brookings consultant.

of the Communications Satellite Corporation, Richard McArdle of the National Institute of Public Affairs, James M. Mitchell of Brookings, Frank Pace, industrial director and consultant, and John A. Perkins of the University of Delaware. The manuscript was also read and commented upon by James W. Davis, Jr., Glenn V. Gibson, Bertrand M. Harding, Walter O. Jacobson, Roger W. Jones, F. P. Kilpatrick, John W. Macy, Jr., Rufus E. Miles, Jr., Frederick C. Mosher, R. Shale Paul, Wallace S. Sayre, Robert F. Steadman, and Robert H. Willey. The Brookings Institution gratefully acknowledges the help of all these persons and organizations. The final draft benefited from the criticisms of a reading committee consisting of Messrs. Kilpatrick, Macy, Mosher, and Rocco C. Siciliano.

Particular thanks are due Chairman John W. Macy, Jr., of the United States Civil Service Commission and his staff, and the personnel directors of federal departments and agencies for their sympathetic and cooperative support of the study.

The Institution appreciates the support of the Ford Foundation, which financed this study.

Mr. Stanley, as the author, is responsible for the accuracy and appropriateness of the statements and interpretations. The views expressed in this report do not purport to represent the views of other staff members, officers, or trustees of the Brookings Institution.

Robert D. Calkins
President

September 1964
The Brookings Institution
1775 Massachusetts Avenue, N. W.
Washington, D. C.

Contents

Foreword vii

1. *Introduction: Key Personnel in the Federal Civil Service* . . 1

2. *Approach and Background* 6

    Criteria for a Higher Civil Service Personnel System 7
    Study Methods 9
    The Manpower Market of the Future 9
    Size and Nature of the Federal Bureaucracy 10
    Responsibility for Federal Personnel Administration 12
    Other Studies Related to the Problem 16

3. *Careers of High-Level Employees* 22

    Characteristics of the Group Studied 23
    Mobility 31
    Advancement 34
    Conclusion 38

4. *Management Views of Federal Personnel Systems* 39

    Views on the Higher Civil Service 39
    Views on other Federal Personnel Systems 48

5. *Employee Views of the Higher Civil Service* 56

    Factors in Employees' Careers 56
    Principal Attitudes Expressed 59
    Why They Stay—Why They Leave 64
    Replacements—Not Considered a Problem 69
    Advice to the Young 70
    Dealing with Substandard Employees 72
    Changes Needed in Personnel Administration 72
    "Anything Else You Would Like To Say?" 77
    Summary 77

6. *What Can Be Done? Analysis of the Findings* 78

    The Needs of the Future 79
    Competition for Professionals and Executives 80
    Evaluating Performance and Potential 84
    Training and Development 86
    Selection 95
    Opportunity To Advance 98
    Movement To Meet Program Needs 102
    Salary Levels 105
    Retention and Utilization 107
    Motivation 109
    Mediocre or Unsatisfactory Personnel 111
    Conclusion 115

7. *Alternative Systems Compared* 116

    Criteria and Assumptions 116
    Possible Patterns Summarized 117
    The Present System as It Is Developing 117
    The Present System—Reinforced and Supplemented 119
    A Higher Civil Service Corps 123
    Agency Corps Systems 126
    Conclusions 127

Appendixes

    A. Survey and Sampling Methods 130
    B. Employees and Former Employees, by Department and
        Agency 136
    C. Major Occupational Fields of Employees and Former
        Employees 137
    D. Highest Level of Education of Employees and Former
        Employees 138

Index 139

1

Introduction: Key Personnel in the Federal Civil Service

THIS IS A BRIEF STUDY of the higher civil service—some 16,000 executives and professionals in grades GS–15 through 18.[1] Their performance is critical in determining the effectiveness and efficiency of the entire government. Their knowledge, their skills, their decisions have far-reaching effects on the welfare and defense of the American people.

These scientific, professional, and managerial employees are those who run the day-to-day affairs of the government—division chiefs, budget officers, laboratory directors, chief attorneys, and many more. Most of them are under regular civil service laws; a few, under special statutes.

This study was made not only because of the importance of these employees but also because of some serious concerns about them: shortages of manpower in key professional, scientific, and managerial occupations; the indifferent "image" of federal employment revealed in a recent Brookings study;[2] and the difficulties which the government experiences in securing and holding talented men in key positions.

Questions about concepts, structure, policies, and procedures govern-

---

[1] Including a few employees not in these grades but paid at equivalent salary levels.

[2] Franklin P. Kilpatrick, Milton C. Cummings, Jr., M. Kent Jennings, *The Image of the Federal Service* (Brookings Institution, 1964), pp. 145–46.

1

ing the higher federal civil service are also implicit in the fact that the federal government performs much of its managerial and professional work through officers employed under different personnel systems: the military services, the Commissioned Corps of the Public Health Service, the Foreign Service, and others. Similar questions arise from the government's widespread use of contracts with private industry to perform research and development work.

The Assignment

The purpose of this study has been to evaluate the personnel system within which the higher civil servants [3] are employed. This has been done by assembling facts about samples of these executives and professionals and by analyzing various judgments about the conditions under which they are chosen and serve. Samples of both present and former employees were studied.

The project design called for a relatively brief study whose results would be presented in a problem paper. This document was to analyze the limitations of present policies, procedures, and institutional concepts in dealing with scientific, professional, and managerial manpower in the federal civil service. It was to concentrate on the realities of 1963 and assess the consequences of alternative courses of action, including inaction.

The Question of Quality

How able are these higher civil servants, how qualified? They are sure of their own competence, and by and large their superiors think they are excellent. Yet valid and reliable indicators of their professional and executive quality are not available—in either absolute or relative terms. It would take a monumental piece of research to obtain agreement on quality standards and then to evaluate federal program managers, attorneys, physicians, insurance experts, or biologists against these standards. Lacking this, one has to refer to broader judgments. Some are favorable, such as that of a prominent industrialist:

[3] The terms "higher civil servants" and "higher civil service" in this study refer to personnel in grades GS–15 through 18.

During the past 15 years, and under three successive administrations, I have been privileged to observe at firsthand the work of our senior career officers, and to do so not only in Washington, but in many of the remote parts of the world. They are the backbone of our Government, and their quality determines in large measure its effectiveness. Among them are some who are careless in the performance of their duties, and some who are mediocre, as there are in business. But there are many, I am proud to say, who are simply superb, equal in every way to the best whom I have known in industry, in the professions, or in any of the other walks of life. It is the merit of these outstanding men that the Pay Panel seeks to recognize and reward in order that more like them may be persuaded to enter the Government service.[4]

Or that of another, who also served in high government posts:

I have found, as have many other business men who have come to Washington, that the large majority of those who choose government employment as a career have a high sense of dedication. Our government is fortunate in having so many men and women of exceptional ability who put their minds and their hearts into their work, frequently under circumstances that their counterparts in business would find extremely discouraging.[5]

Others are less favorable:

Ralph Budd, manufacturer and railroad president, who also served in a business capacity for the Government, offers as a general comment: "One of the serious problems of government is the tendency of bureaucratic workers to continually build their staffs and 'carry their empires' far beyond the actual needs of the situation."[6]

Appalling mediocrity pervades the entire top echelons of the U.S. federal service. What I see looks terribly serious and terribly dangerous. Drastic steps must be taken to find a remedy—otherwise this country will suffer great harm.[7]

The present study necessarily relied upon quality judgments from

[4] Clarence B. Randall, "U.S. Problem: Low Pay for Top Jobs," *New York Times Magazine*, Sept. 15, 1963, p. 93.

[5] Meyer Kestnbaum, quoted in "Career Administrators in Government Service," *Good Government*, Vol. LXXIV, No. 3 (May-June 1957), p. 27.

[6] Robert B. Curry (Vice President and Comptroller of Southern Railway System), "The Public Administrator as a Professional Manager—As Viewed by Private Industry," *Advanced Management*, Vol. 24, No. 12 (December 1959), p. 19.

[7] Remarks by a leading foundation official, paraphrased by Kenneth O. Warner in *Personnel Man*, Vol. 10, No. 1 (January 1964), p. 4.

inside the government service—judgments that were mostly favorable, as might be expected.

What This Study Shows

This report analyzes the operation of the higher federal civil service with reference to criteria of an effective personnel system. This is done after review of some background considerations of government organization and of results of other studies. (See Chapter 2.)

FACTS ABOUT THE GROUP. Most of the group studied are in their forties or fifties and have served in the government from 15 to 30 years. A majority are eligible to retire in 5 or 10 years, and about half of the total plan to do so. Their careers show little occupational, geographical, or organizational mobility, but steady advancement. They took about 20 years to reach their present grades. Most are college graduates: 83 percent have bachelor's degrees, and 33 percent, advanced degrees. Those who left government service did so after an average of 22 years of service. (See Chapter 3.)

MANAGEMENT'S VIEWS. Interviews of high management officials throughout the government revealed reasonable satisfaction with their ability to attract and keep superior employees in the higher grades. They showed concern, however, about inadequate manpower forecasting and inflexible salary administration, among other things. (See Chapter 4.)

VIEWS OF EMPLOYEES AND FORMER EMPLOYEES. Members and former members of the higher civil service were generally well satisfied with their careers, largely because of the public importance and interest of their work. They had a high opinion of the effectiveness of their agencies and of the competence of their colleagues. Their dissatisfactions centered around "red tape"—administrative delay and inflexibility. They believed that executives and professionals leave the service for higher salaries. They had many different suggestions for improving personnel administration at higher levels—primarily speedier recruiting, more flexible assignment, and less rigid classification and pay administration. (See Chapter 5.)

EVALUATION OF THE PRESENT PERSONNEL SYSTEM. The federal personnel system for the higher civil service, viewed as a whole, has been fairly effective. Viewing the service against present demands, there is reason for satisfaction. Nevertheless, significant improvements should be made in forecasting needs, recruiting at middle and top levels, evaluating employees, long-term training, interorganization developmental assignments, pay flexibility, and means of dealing with mediocre employees. (See Chapter 6.)

WEIGHING OF ALTERNATIVE SYSTEMS. The present system as it is developing is considered in comparison with three major alternatives: a "beefed-up" version of the present system, with several new features; a governmentwide corps system for the higher civil service; and separate agency corps systems. There is a clear need, under any system, for ever stronger Presidential leadership in personnel administration. (See Chapter 7.)

Next Steps

This report concludes that many innovations are needed if the higher civil service system is to achieve real progress. Officials of the Executive Office of the President, of the Civil Service Commission, and of other agencies might weigh the data and judgments in this study against other administrative, economic, and political factors. Some of the possible courses of action would require consideration by Congress.

Regardless of what choices are made, there must be continuing positive action. The progress now being made by the Civil Service Commission and by the agencies in their executive and professional personnel programs should be regarded as an absolute minimum.

Higher civil service employees with superior technical ability, breadth of viewpoint, and sureness of judgment will always be needed to meet the government's commitments in both domestic and international fields. The higher civil service personnel program must be an ever developing one. Those who are responsible for it can take pride in their achievements, but they can never be truly satisfied. They must set their sights on a rising target and hold to it.

2

Approach and Background

THIS STUDY brings together facts and judgments about the careers of top federal executives and professionals. The findings and discussion are related to several criteria for judging the effectiveness of a personnel system.

Before the criteria are stated, it is necessary to indicate the kind of people the system should recruit, develop, and retain. The scope and impact of their responsibilities demand that they be *superior professionals and executives*—not merely adequate ones. They will have to direct complex programs of political, economic, and social importance. They will have to influence officials of foreign governments and of various levels of American government. They will have to provide leadership to government contractors who employ other high-caliber people. And as scientists, professionals, or executives they must demonstrate skill and knowledge that will command the respect of the top men in their fields.

Most higher federal civil servants operate in dynamic and extremely fragmented fields. They must therefore have flexibility, a high innovative capacity, a sharp critical faculty, and ability to synthesize and integrate. They must be persons of broad experience and broad intellectual interests. They must be able to "get things done" on schedule, with adequate thoroughness but without overrefinement. They must be able to deal effectively with Congress, with influential clientele groups, with the general public, and with one another. They must be willing to take responsibility and to be accountable for their actions.

No personnel system is likely to find a civil servant who has all these superlative qualities. The system should be able, however, to provide balanced teams of employees who are superior in the combinations of qualities needed.

Criteria for a Higher Civil Service Personnel System

The following criteria were developed from the standard literature of public personnel administration and from discussions with practitioners in that field. They are a distillation of present-day thinking as to best practices. Other analysts might change the criteria in order, emphasis, or detail, but would probably not vary the basic content significantly. A system meeting these criteria should—

1. Analyze future needs for higher personnel and evaluate prospects of meeting such needs.
    a. Forecast needs five years ahead in quantity and in quality by organization and by occupation.
    b. Inventory and evaluate present personnel against future needs.
2. Compete successfully with other employers for superior personnel.
3. Make systematic, reliable, and valid evaluations of employees' performance and potential—as a basis for development and promotion.
4. Develop and train enough superior employees to fill most higher jobs—employees whose professional skills are excellent and up to date and whose perspectives are broad and mature.
5. Select the best candidates from a reasonably broad area of consideration for promotion or appointment to higher jobs—with reference to the particular needs of each job.
6. Provide advancement in compensation at a rate consistent with
    a. The employee's professional development.
    b. Rates of advancement offered by competing employers.
7. Provide flexibility of assignment to meet needs of the program and also changing circumstances of the employee.
8. Compensate personnel at fair market value for their services.

9. Retain and use to fullest advantage those employees who make a valuable contribution to organization goals.
10. Motivate personnel to give a full measure of cooperative effort.
11. Shift substandard personnel to jobs they can do effectively or discharge them.

Differences in Careers

The personnel system must adapt itself to a variety of professional and executive careers. Each type of career must provide reasonable promise of intellectual and professional growth and of advancement in responsibility, pay, and recognition.

Yet careers differ widely in the amount of specialized knowledge they require and in the extent of advance preparation needed. They differ in the number of organizations in which they may exist. (Few agencies employ foresters.) They differ also in the extent to which they lead to other career opportunities. (Law and engineering may lead to high executive posts; chemistry usually does not. Tax lawyers and electronic technicians can easily get jobs outside the government; many administrative officers cannot.)

Where a career is limited to one agency, it is reasonable to expect that agency to provide opportunities for development and recognition that will make up for the lack of mobility. To the extent that circumstances in the agency prevent recognition, development, and advancement for employees, a decline in quality of staff may be expected.

Organizational Provisions

A model system must also provide organizational arrangements to achieve its goals. In the federal agencies there must be professional personnel staffs to help executives find, employ, develop, assign, and make best use of their personnel. There must be a strong central personnel organization to provide technical leadership to the agency staffs, to supply needed central services, and to maintain protection for employees against unjust actions. There must be effective communication between the agencies, the central personnel organization, the President, and the Congress.

Study Methods

Various methods were used to assess the values and defects of the higher federal civil service system.[1] First, a review was made of reports of other relevant studies and of other literature in this field. These reports are summarized in the final section of this chapter.

Second, 100 executives of departments and agencies were interviewed to obtain "management" judgments on higher civil service policies and programs.

Third, more than 150 employees in grades GS–15 through 18 were interviewed to find out how well their own career goals had been met in federal service.

Fourth, about 100 employees and 100 former employees (who had left the service in the last three years) answered questionnaires.

Fifth, statistical analyses were made of personal and career data for nearly 400 present employees and nearly 200 former employees.

Finally, there were seven group meetings at which informed persons discussed the issues in this study.

The present report reflects the findings of all these research activities.

Before specific findings and analyses are discussed, it will be helpful to review background factors about federal personnel administration and to summarize some other studies related to this one.

The Manpower Market of the Future

In the foreseeable future the federal government will continue to compete with commerce and industry for personnel possessing skills that are now scarce and will continue to be scarce—such as scientists, engineers, mathematicians, auditors, and experts in systems design and data processing. The government's competitive position will be better than it was because of the 1964 salary increases and because the market for such personnel is easing a little as government procurement is cut down. Nevertheless, trend analyses generally show long-term shortages

[1] See Appendix A for more detail on the survey and sampling methodology of this study.

in these fields. At present it is uncertain whether the educational system can meet these shortages. They will be mitigated, but not really solved, by in-service training, outside training assignments, and personnel utilization improvements.

Trends in college majors indicate that graduates in the social sciences and humanities will be available in greatly increasing numbers. These "generalists" can be trained to take their places in the higher federal civil service of the future. If the federal government is to attract its share of able young people in the future it must arrange stepped-up "selling" programs in high schools as well as in colleges.[2]

It will be difficult for the federal service to attract high-quality executives or specialists from private industry in midcareer or late career. By then they will be well "locked in" by compensation and fringe benefit systems, and their potential interest in the public service will have faded. A few may be available, however, to start new careers with the federal government when they retire from their present employment in their sixties or to shift careers earlier.

The federal service is likely to continue to stay ahead of other employers in its willingness to hire and promote underutilized groups— women, Negroes, and handicapped persons—but extra effort will be needed to make these groups into significant sources of upper-level manpower.

Size and Nature of the Federal Bureaucracy

Size and Occupational Variety

The federal civil service has changed little in total number over the last 10 years: 2.369 million in 1953, 2.225 million in 1958, 2.361 million in 1963, and 2.346 million in 1964.[3] The number does not seem likely to increase significantly in the next ten years, assuming no major change in the economy or in the temperature of the Cold War. There will be

---

[2] Franklin P. Kilpatrick, Milton C. Cummings, Jr., M. Kent Jennings, *The Image of the Federal Service* (Brookings Institution, 1964), p. 252.

[3] Paid civilian employment in the executive branch in the states, territories, and possessions as of the end of the fiscal years. Source: annual reports of the U. S. Civil Service Commission.

needs and demands for new and expanded services to the increasing population, but these payroll-increasing pressures will be checked by increasing automation of operations and by counterpressures to contract out federal services and to hold the line on federal employment.

Despite the stability in size of the federal service there is substantial attrition and replacement. In calendar year 1963 total accessions and separations both approached 20 percent.

Nor can any material change be foreseen in the great occupational variety of the federal bureaucracy. Few services are likely to be reduced or discontinued. Those which are performed for Uncle Sam by state or local governments or by private industry will still have to be supervised and checked by federal experts. And the growing variety and complexity of government programs will continue to show the need for persons of flexibility and high learning capacity in federal service.

Characteristics

A few other characteristics of the federal bureaucracy are relevant to this study:

1. It is an *open* service—that is, entry can take place at many different levels.[4] Most of the higher civil servants, however, entered at relatively low levels.

2. The *merit principle* is accepted throughout most of the service when this term is interpreted to mean *resistance to partisan political patronage*. Competition for many positions has become limited, however, as a result of decentralization of authority for personnel decisions.

3. *Individual employee initiative* plays an important part in decisions on training, transfer, and promotion. Employees are frequently able to arrange placements for themselves.

4. The federal service tends to be *self-governing and self-perpetuating*. The political executives in any agency make few personnel decisions themselves, and they are inexperienced in many of the details of agency operation. This leaves administration largely in the hands of career civil servants.

---

[4] Certain agency personnel systems within the civil service (such as that of the Forest Service) are virtually closed services above the entry level.

Responsibility for Federal Personnel Administration

The Role of Congress

Congress has made infrequent *major* changes in the basic legislative structure of federal personnel administration: the Civil Service Act (1883), the Classification Act (1923), the Retirement Act (1920), the Veterans' Preference Act (1944), and legislation governing leave (1884), group insurance benefits (1954), training (1958), and health benefits (1959). The legislative branch has made clear its intention to continue to control this structure, particularly salary levels. In a typical year there are minor amendments to these laws, but real overhauls are infrequent. The interests of Congress "tend to focus upon the rank-and-file of the civil service, not upon its higher ranks or the more specialized leadership groups." [5] Interest in post offices and postal employees tends to color congressional committee attitudes toward all federal employment.

In general, Congress has tended to accept the basic personnel system, to become increasingly liberal with pay and with fringe benefits, and to display increasing approval of employee training activities. [6]

The Role of the President

From time to time Presidents have extended the civil service system or brought about improvements in personnel administration or have spoken out on matters involving the public service. For the most part, however, their leadership in federal personnel matters has been sporadic. Continuing leadership has been left to the Civil Service Commission and to agency heads. Yet major changes have always reflected Presidential leadership or support (e.g., Franklin Roosevelt's extension of civil service coverage and appointment of agency personnel directors; Truman's support of substantial Classification Act amend-

[5] Wallace S. Sayre, "The Public Service," in *Goals for Americans*, Report of the President's Commission on National Goals (Prentice-Hall, 1960), p. 288.

[6] For a critical review of congressional interest in the civil service, see Joseph P. Harris, *Congressional Control of Administration* (Brookings Institution, 1964), pp. 163–203.

ments; Eisenhower's sponsorship of fringe benefits; and the Kennedy-Johnson backing of salary comparability).

Beginning with the administration of Franklin Roosevelt, the White House has included a liaison office for personnel management, which might have been expected to aid in providing real leadership for federal personnel administration. Except during the Eisenhower Administration this office had little perceptible impact on personnel matters.[7] During the first part of that Administration, Philip Young, who served as the President's assistant for personnel management as well as Chairman of the Civil Service Commission, exerted considerable influence in sponsorship of new fringe-benefit legislation, in drawing new boundaries between career and political jobs, in coordination of personnel policies covering overseas employees, and in other important areas of personnel administration.

His successor, Rocco C. Siciliano (he wore only the White House hat), was involved in a number of significant personnel developments, including military pay increases, the proposed program of the Career Executive Committee and Board, the health benefits program, and the beginning of pay studies which ultimately resulted in the salary reform legislation enacted in the Kennedy Administration.[8]

President Kennedy did not have an assistant for personnel management, although he did use a full-time specialist in recruitment for hard-to-fill noncareer positions.

The President's interest in personnel matters is also served by a small staff in the Bureau of the Budget's Office of Management and Organization. This group provides staff advice and studies on personnel matters that require action by the Bureau or the President, particularly those involving new legislation. Its scope includes all federal personnel systems, not just the civil service.

A need for a special organization to help the President exercise personnel leadership for higher-level personnel is stated by Sayre:

> The President needs in his own office an agency for personnel leadership—especially for attention to the personnel policies and procedures affecting the higher ranks of the Executive Branch—

[7] Indeed, during the Truman Administration it doubled as a patronage office.
[8] See Steering Committee of the Interdepartmental Committee on Civilian Compensation, *Report on Civilian Compensation in the Executive Branch of the Government* (1957).

which would possess status, responsibility and resources comparable to those of the Budget Bureau and the Council of Economic Advisers. This personnel agency should prepare annually, or even more frequently, a Presidential message to the Congress and to the public, reporting on the quality, the accomplishments, and the difficulties of the federal personnel systems and recommending measures for their improvement.[9]

The same point is made among the recommendations of the Kilpatrick-Cummings-Jennings "federal image" study:

It should be recognized, openly and explicitly, that the President of the United States has special responsibility for upper-level career employees. Employees in the lower echelons, because of their numbers and the availability to them of union representation, will rarely fail to receive sympathetic attention from Congress. The facts of political life make it unlikely that Congress will demonstrate in legislation a similar concern for the upper echelons unless their needs receive strong support from the President. One would think that a simple concern for the effectiveness of the Executive branch would cause the President to give high priority to this matter. However, in the past, presidential support has been sporadic and too often given simply in response to impending crises or glaring inequities. When the Chief Executive fails to assume special responsibility for comprehensive planning and continuous strong support of measures designed to enhance the welfare, quality, and performance of upper-level career employees, it is an abdication of a major presidential responsibility, and should be regarded as such.[10]

The need for institutionalizing Presidential personnel leadership is discussed further in Chapter 7.

The Role of the Civil Service Commission

The work of the Civil Service Commission combines three kinds of functions: [11]

1. *Control and enforcement* (e.g., review of agency personnel func-

---

[9] Sayre, *op. cit.*, p. 289.

[10] Kilpatrick *et al., op. cit.*, p. 267.

[11] The term "Civil Service Commission" is used here to mean that agency, not the three Commissioners. Most of the executive powers of the agency were vested in its Chairman by Reorganization Plan No. 5 of 1949, with the Commissioners retaining rule-making and appellate functions.

tions carried out under delegated authority; approval of qualifications and classification in certain cases; administration of the Veterans' Preference Act and the Hatch Act; issuance of regulations; adjudication of employee appeals).

2. *Service* (e.g., centralized examining for certain positions; conducting security checks; administration of retirement, life insurance, and health benefits laws).

3. Positive *leadership* in federal personnel administration (e.g., development of new training programs, recruitment activities, salary reform plans, and personnel research).

The Commission's programs have developed impressively in all three areas in the last decade—particularly in the third function, which is most relevant to the conclusions of this study. The Commission has helped bring about salary increases and reforms; required the establishment of merit promotion programs; started a central placement roster of "supergrade" employees; established a variety of executive training programs, including the beginning of a "staff college" facility at Kings Point, New York; and expanded its public information program on federal careers. Other program developments could be cited.

It is appropriate to question whether this personnel program leadership can achieve as much as the government needs to achieve as long as it is linked with more traditional civil service activities:

> . . . we must take a very hard and critical look at the present arrangement which places in the hands of the CSC both the regulatory function and the major responsibility for government-wide stimulation of new and positive personnel philosophies and practices. The two functions are seldom complementary—and in fact often antagonistic —both in their operational aspects and in the outlook they require of those who administer them. Furthermore, it is difficult for the people who must deal with the CSC to give full appreciation and weight to its positive functions. Its historical regulatory mission— and its continuing regulatory responsibilities—are bound to condition their view, and, in many cases, cause them to adopt a questioning or suspicious attitude. Finally, there is the very important question of whether leadership in personnel matters, which is an important executive function, ought not to be in the Office of the Chief Executive, rather than in the hands of a so-called independent agency.[12]

[12] Kilpatrick, *et al., op. cit.,* p. 268.

The Role of the Agency Head

Despite the influence of the Congress, the President, and the Commission, everyday personnel administration is in the hands of department and agency heads. They and their subordinate executives recruit, select, train, transfer, classify, promote, and discharge. There are limitations on their discretion: Some of their actions, such as classifying "supergrade" positions (GS-16, 17, and 18), must be approved by the Civil Service Commission. Other actions, such as discharges for cause, may be appealed to the Commission. Their personnel activities are inspected by the Commission's staff. In general, however, the agency head has the power to run his own personnel program.

This independence is both a virtue and a necessity, considering the huge scope and variety of government programs. These programs must be managed in workable pieces, and personnel administration is an inseparable part of management. Each agency can develop personnel activities which are appropriate to its operating programs. Yet the independence also has disadvantages. Agency personnel programs may vary in progressiveness (see Chapter 4). The separateness may also result in missed opportunities to do the best possible personnel job for the government as a whole (see Chapter 6).

Other Studies Related to the Problem

In the past decade higher federal personnel have been the subject of frequent special studies and of much professional literature. This emphasis resulted in part from increased attention to "executive development" in private industry. It was also a consequence of increasing competition for scarce skills and for people of top ability, at a time when federal programs were expanding and when special skills were being required by new programs.

The American Assembly Report (1954)

First of the significant studies of federal personnel in the 1950's and 1960's was the study of the Sixth American Assembly, with background papers prepared by experts and a final report expressing the consensus of the distinguished citizens who participated in the discussions. This report endorsed the rank-in-man principle, use of a central interagency transfer unit, special identification of civil servants of demonstrated competence, more systematic appraisal of employees, higher salaries, and stepped-up training and development programs.[13]

The Second Hoover Commission (1955)

The reports on personnel and civil service by the Second Hoover Commission and by its task force assigned to this subject were a prime stimulus to discussion and further study of the higher civil service.[14] The reports covered a wide range of topics: the division between political and career executives, recruitment, conflict of interest, compensation, training, separation, and many others. They were best known, however, for their recommendation that a Senior Civil Service be established. This was to be a specially selected corps of highly qualified administrators with personal rank, free from politics, and able to move from one agency to another to meet program needs. The proposal was widely discussed and debated, both informally and in the literature of public personnel administration.[15]

[13] The American Assembly, *The Federal Government Service: Its Character, Prestige, and Problems* (Graduate School of Business, Columbia University, 1954).

[14] Commission on Organization of the Executive Branch of the Government, *Personnel and Civil Service* (Government Printing Office, 1955), pp. 37–44; and the Commission's Task Force on Personnel and Civil Service, *Report on Personnel and Civil Service* (Government Printing Office, 1955), pp. 49–62.

[15] See, for example:

Leonard D. White, "The Senior Civil Service," *Public Administration Review,* Vol. 15 (Autumn 1955), pp. 237–43.

———, "The Case for the Senior Civil Service," *Personnel Administration,* Vol. 19 (January–February 1956), pp. 4–9.

Herman M. Somers, "Some Reservations About the Senior Civil Service," *Personnel Administration,* Vol. 19 (January–February 1956), pp. 10–18.

Everett Reimer, "The Case Against the Senior Civil Service," *Personnel Administration,* Vol. 19 (March–April 1956), pp. 31–40.

Paul P. Van Riper, "The Senior Civil Service and the Career System," *Public Administration Review,* Vol. 18 (Summer 1958), pp. 189–200.

William Pincus, "The Opposition to the Senior Civil Service," *Public Administration Review,* Vol. 18 (Autumn 1958), pp. 324–31.

The Career Executive Committee and Board (1957–1959)

The Senior Civil Service proposal of the Hoover Commission was viewed with apprehension or distaste by the more articulate of its intended beneficiaries, and federal personnel officers filled its image with needles. Nevertheless, President Eisenhower set up a Career Executive Committee in 1957 to make recommendations to him on the Hoover Commission proposal. This committee recommended, and the President established, a Career Executive Board. The Board prepared tentative regulations providing for inclusion of designated "supergrade" positions in a "Career Executive Service"; designation of certain employees as "Career Executives"; and a roster of "Career Executive Eligibles." Employees were under no obligation to become "Career Executives," nor were agency heads to be required to use "Career Executives" or to have their personnel authority limited in any way.[16] The Board was terminated in 1959 when congressional appropriation subcommittees denied it support.

Ultimately, however, some of the proposals of the Career Executive Committee and the Career Executive Board went into effect. A career executive placement roster was set up, salary levels were increased, regulatory restrictions on the quotas of "supergrade" positions were reduced, and many executive development courses were conducted at government expense.

The David-Pollock Study

The Paul David–Ross Pollock book *Executives for Government* (1957), like the Hoover Commission report, dealt with political executives as well as career civil servants.[17] Its treatment of the latter included evaluation of several variants of the Senior Civil Service concept from the viewpoints of the employees themselves, the President, the Congress, and the public. This book presented no recommendations but sought mainly to give perspective and to weigh alternatives.

---

[16] Career Executive Board, *Report of Activities for Period March 4, 1958, to June 30, 1959.* (Mimeo.)

[17] Paul T. David and Ross Pollock, *Executives for Government* (Brookings Institution, 1957).

Studies on Scientists and Engineers

In 1957 the "Philip Young Committee" reviewed employment policies affecting federal scientists and engineers and recommended increased salaries, removal of restrictions on "supergrade" jobs, increased training outside the government, improved agency promotion programs, and use of interagency placement rosters.[18] These recommendations have now become established practice.

At the same time the "Cordiner Committee" on professional and technical personnel in the Department of Defense also recommended higher compensation, more flexibility in "supergrade" classification, and establishment of an elite corps of scientists and engineers in the Department.[19]

More recently the Federal Council for Science and Technology issued a pair of reports on personnel administration affecting scientists and engineers. One provided evidence of the severe salary competition for such employees.[20] The other dealt with laboratory organization and management, recruitment, leave, relocation expenses, and other employment matters.[21]

Studies of Other Personnel Systems

Two studies of the Foreign Service in the Department of State pointed up the need for improved plans and procedures for selection and best use of specialized personnel. The "Wriston Report" of 1954 dealt mainly with the need for better integration of the civil service with the foreign service. It also stressed stepped-up recruitment, im-

[18] Committee on Scientists and Engineers for Federal Government Programs, *A Report to the President with Recommendations for the Improved Personnel Management of Scientists and Engineers in the Federal Service* (April 1957).

[19] *Report of the Defense Advisory Committee on Professional and Technical Compensation*, Vol. II, *Civilian Personnel* (Government Printing Office, May 1957).

[20] Federal Council for Science and Technology, *The Competition for Quality: The Effect of Current Salary Levels on the Federal Government's Ability to Recruit and Retain Superior Scientific and Engineering Personnel* (January 1962).

[21] Federal Council for Science and Technology, *The Competition for Quality: Non-Salary Factors Affecting the Selection, Recruitment, Development, and Retention of Superior Personnel in the Scientific Service of the Federal Government* (April 1962).

proved planning and administration of promotion programs, increased training, and particularly more attentive and continuous leadership from top management.[22]

Eight years later much of the same ground was replowed by the "Herter Committee," with the furrow widened to include the Agency for International Development and the United States Information Agency. Among the Committee's many positive proposals were better forecasting of personnel needs; improved evaluation of employees; more vigorous recruitment; increased hiring above junior levels; inter-agency assignments of senior officers; and more effective selection-out practices.[23]

Another relevant study was that made of the commissioned and civil service personnel of the Public Health Service by an expert advisory committee, headed by Marion Folsom, former Secretary of Health, Education, and Welfare.[24] The committee's report stressed the need for better leadership, coordination, and organization of both personnel systems, forecasts of manpower needs, continuous recruiting, a career development program, and increased pay.

"The American Federal Executive"

The recent book *The American Federal Executive* contains copious information on the characteristics of a large sample of federal executives in grades GS–14 and up.[25] Their origins, education, career mobility, and progression are developed in considerable detail. The findings of that study are compared with results of the present study in Chapter 3.

"The Image of the Federal Service"

The recent study of the image of the federal service by Kilpatrick, Cummings, and Jennings contains much useful information about the

[22] *Toward a Stronger Foreign Service: Report of the Secretary of State's Public Committee on Personnel* (Government Printing Office, June 1954).

[23] *Personnel for the New Diplomacy: Report of the Committee on Foreign Affairs Personnel* (Carnegie Endowment for International Peace, December 1962).

[24] *Report of the Advisory Committee on Public Health Service Personnel Systems* (U. S. Department of Health, Education, and Welfare, March 1962).

[25] W. Lloyd Warner, Paul P. Van Riper, Norman H. Martin, and Orvis F. Collins, *The American Federal Executive* (Yale University Press, 1963).

aspirations and perceptions of federal executives, scientists, and engineers.[26] Some of that study's findings are discussed later (see Chapter 5).

CED Report

Finally, many of the issues discussed in the present study were also explored in a recent statement by the Research and Policy Committee of the Committee for Economic Development.[27] This statement recommends increased salaries for the higher civil service; establishment of two new, higher pay grades; increased flexibility of transfers within the government and of exchange of personnel between government and business; and other changes. Of particular interest is its recommendation that an Office of Executive Personnel be created in the White House.

[26] Kilpatrick et al., op. cit.
[27] Improving Executive Management in the Federal Government (Committee for Economic Development, 1964).

3

Careers of High-Level Employees

THE TYPICAL FEDERAL CIVIL SERVANT covered by this study is a man of 50, working in Washington. He is a college graduate. He started in grade GS–9. He has 23 years of continuous federal service, and he took 20 of those years to reach his present grade. He has had a relatively stable career, working in no more than one or two occupational fields. He has also been employed in only one or two departments or agencies. As Chapter 5 shows, he is generally well satisfied but has some definite ideas on how his employment could be improved.

The data in the present chapter about the employees' personal characteristics, mobility, and advancement were taken from official government personnel records. (See Appendix A for an explanation of the methodology.)

Comparisons are made, as appropriate, with information contained in the following studies:

1. The 1959–63 study of federal executives made by Warner, Van Riper, Martin, and Collins.[1] This covered federal executives in grades GS–14 and higher, and data are as of mid-1959.

2. A study by John J. Corson, of Princeton University, tentatively titled *The Role of Top-Level Civil Servants*. This study, which has not yet been published, contains mid-1963 data for federal employees in grades GS–16 through 18 and those scientists and engineers covered by Public Law 313.

[1] W. Lloyd Warner, Paul P. Van Riper, Norman H. Martin, and Orvis F. Collins. *The American Federal Executive* (Yale University Press, 1963).

22

3. Tabulations by the U. S. Civil Service Commission of characteristics of employees on the Career Executive Roster (mostly grades GS–16 through 18) in 1962 and 1963.

Characteristics of the Group Studied

Number of Men and Women

Only one of the 363 present employees and three of the 196 former employees are women. The smallness of the number is significant, but the present study does not include any research on sex discrimination.[2]

Agencies and Locations

About two-thirds of the group were employed in headquarters offices; one-third in the field. (This was true of both present and former employees.)

Divided by types of departments and agencies, the group fell into these categories (N is the number of persons covered):

	(N = 559)
Department of Defense (including military departments)	27.2%
Other Cabinet departments	34.3
Other agencies	38.5
	100.0

Forty-three percent of the Defense employees were in the field, as were 21 percent of employees of other Cabinet departments and 37 percent of those from other agencies. Detailed figures on the number and percent of the sample in individual departments and agencies appear in Appendix B.

[2] Career patterns for women are discussed in Chapter 11 of the Warner–Van Riper study. See also *American Women: Report of the President's Commission on the Status of Women* (1963), pp. 31–34; and Evelyn Harrison, "The Working Woman: Barriers in Employment," *Public Administration Review*, Vol. 24 (June 1964), pp. 78–85.

Grades

The classification grades of the sample were in the usual pyramid form, but the pyramid for the former employees has a broader base and sharper apex:

GRADE	PRESENT EMPLOYEES (N = 363)	FORMER EMPLOYEES (N = 196)	TOTAL (N = 559)
GS-18	9.6%	4.1%	7.7%
GS-17	14.9	5.6	11.6
GS-16	27.0	13.8	22.4
GS-15	37.8	70.4	49.2
P.L. 313	7.4	1.5	5.4
Other	3.3	4.6	3.7
	100.0	100.0	100.0

Occupations

Those in scientific and engineering occupations totaled 38.5 percent; in other occupations, 61.5 percent. Appendix C shows in detail the "major occupational fields" of the group studied.

Date of Entry into Federal Service

About half of the group studied entered federal service during or before the New Deal, while the other half were appointed during and after World War II:

PERIOD OF ENTRY INTO FEDERAL SERVICE	PRESENT EMPLOYEES [3] (N = 363)	FORMER EMPLOYEES (N = 195) [4]	TOTAL (N = 558) [4]
Before 1933	13.8%	30.8%	19.7%
1933–1940	36.4	21.0	31.0
1941–1945	23.1	11.3	19.0
1946–1952	19.3	18.5	19.0
1953–1960	5.8	13.8	8.6
1961–1963	1.6	4.6	2.7

[3] These entry periods agree closely with those shown for present employees in the Corson study.

[4] Throughout this book N's will vary slightly according to the number of useable responses received.

Present Employees: Age, Length of Service

AGE AT PRESENT. The median age of present employees studied is 50. This agrees substantially with the Corson study (covering only "super-grades" and P.L. 313's), which showed a mean age of 52. The latter figure was also the median age of employees on the Career Executive Roster.[5] The "average age" of the Warner–Van Riper sample (which included GS–14's) was 49.6.[6]

Of the employees covered by the present study 30 percent are 55 or over; 55.2 percent are 50 or over; and 82.3 percent, 45 or over. (See Chart 3.1.) Detailed age groupings look like this:

AGE	(N) = 362
Under 25	—
25–29	0.3%
30–34	0.3
35–39	5.5
40–44	11.6
45–49	27.1
50–54	25.1
55–59	18.8
60–64	10.2
65–69	0.8
70 and over	0.3
	100.0

The modes between age 45 and 55 are consistent with the Civil Service Commission data.[7]

AGE AT ENTRY INTO SERVICE. As one would expect, the higher civil servants first entered federal service at a relatively early age—28, on the average.[8] The Warner–Van Riper study also shows an "average age" of 28 at entry.[9] About 36 percent started under age 25; 32 percent from 25 to 29; and 14 percent from 30 to 34.

[5] Mel H. Bolster, *Federal Career Executives: Three Years' Experience with the Career Executive Roster* (unpublished manuscript, April 1964), p. 5.

[6] Warner *et al., op. cit.,* p. 386.

[7] "Most career executives in the federal government are between 45 and 55 years of age (median is 52) with from 15 to 30 years of federal service." Bolster, *op. cit.,* p. 5.

[8] Twenty-eight is both mean and median.

[9] Warner *et al., op. cit.,* p. 166.

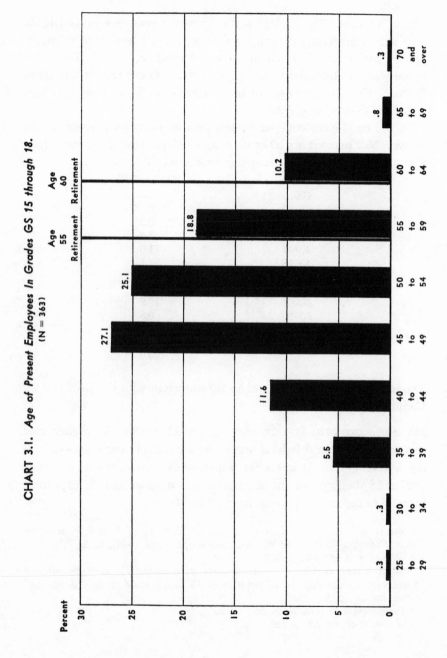

CHART 3.1. Age of Present Employees In Grades GS 15 through 18.
(N = 363)

LENGTH OF SERVICE. The median length of federal service for present employees is 23 years.[10] Almost 37 percent have 25 or more years of service; about 14 percent have 30 or more. (Corson's figures are presented for comparison in Table 3.1)

TABLE 3.1. *Years of Federal Service of Present Employees (Brookings and Corson Studies)*

Years of Service [a]	Brookings (N = 359)	Corson (N = 424)
Under 5	0.9%	8.2%
5–9	4.7	5.2
10–14	7.5	10.9
15–19	13.9	15.8
20–24	36.2	23.6
25–29	23.1	21.9
30–34	7.0	8.7
35 and over	6.7	5.7
	100.0	100.0

[a] An analysis of length of service was also made by departmental and occupational groups for the total sample (both present and former employees). It showed a median of 22 years for Department of Defense employees, as compared to 24.5 for other Cabinet departments, and 22 for other agencies. Scientists and engineers had a shorter median period of service (20 years) than others (24 years).

READINESS TO RETIRE. The typical employee studied is eligible to retire in 7 years, when he will have completed 30 years of service; he will be almost 58 years old then. Two out of every five could retire now, and three out of four will be able to do so in 5 years, as shown by the following percentages:

	(N = 362)
ELIGIBLE TO RETIRE NOW	
Age 55 or more with 30 years or more of service [11]	40.3%
Age 60 or more with 30 years or more of service	18.2
ELIGIBLE TO RETIRE IN 5 YEARS	
Age 50 or more with 25 years or more of service	76.5
Age 55 or more with 25 years or more of service [11]	47.5

[10] Using official service computation dates. Thus military service is included.

[11] Those who are not yet 60 at time of retirement would receive a slightly reduced annuity.

INTENTIONS TO RETIRE. Employees who were interviewed or who filled out questionnaires were asked about their plans to retire. Their replies (although many were not easy to interpret) can be summarized as follows:

	(N = 259)
Plan to retire in:	
Less than 5 years	21.2%
6–10 years	22.0
11–15 years	6.2
16–20 years	2.3
21–25 years	0.8
(Average: 7.03 years)	(52.5)
No plans	30.5
No answer	17.0
	100.0

Very few of the employees in their forties indicated any retirement plans. About two-thirds of those in their fifties reported plans to retire in periods ranging from 2 to 10 years. These "intentions," considered with the eligibility data of those expressing them, suggest that about half of the employees in these grades will leave federal service in 5 to 10 years.

CONCLUSION. The data presented show that a large majority (73 percent) of the present employees came into federal service during the depression of the 1930's, the New Deal, and World War II, when incentives for public service, compared with other employment, seemed more persuasive than now. Most of these employees are middle-aged. About half of them can be expected to retire in 5 to 10 years. An undetermined number of the rest will die, become disabled, or resign. *The government will face a serious problem in replacing these employees,* although many of them and many of their superiors (see Chapters 4 and 5) do not consider it serious.

Former Employees: Age and Length of Service

Fifty-five was the median age at which the former employees studied left federal service. Note, however, that the late forties and early sixties proved to be the modal ages for leaving federal service, as shown on the following page:

AGE AT TIME OF RESIGNATION OR RETIREMENT	(N = 194)
Under 25	—
25–29	—
30–34	3.1%
35–39	10.8
40–44	8.2
45–49	16.0
50–54	9.8
55–59	12.9
60–64	19.1
65–69	13.9
70 and over	6.2
	100.0

(Responses to questionnaires, discussed in Chapter 5, showed "new opportunities" to be a significant reason for leaving in the forties, and retirement to be a leading cause in the sixties.)

Length of service at time of separation showed a fairly even distribution, with 21 years the median length of service:

YEARS OF FEDERAL SERVICE AT TIME OF RESIGNATION OR RETIREMENT	(N = 178)
Under 5	6.8%
5–9	10.1
10–14	12.4
15–19	15.7
20–24	14.0
25–29	14.0
30–34	10.1
35 and over	16.9
	100.0

DATE OF SEPARATION. Most of the former employees had left federal service in recent years, as shown by the following percentages:

DATE OF SEPARATION	(N = 196)
Fiscal Year 1963	22.6%
1962	47.7
1961	27.7
Earlier	2.0
	100.0

Prior Occupations

Some 31 percent of the total group studied had worked for private business or industry before entering government service. Twenty-four percent had been students. The only other significant prior employment was with educational institutions, namely, 13 percent. As might be expected, the percentage of scientific or engineering employees who had worked for educational institutions was higher—18 percent.

Education

LEVEL. Five out of every six of the persons studied had college degrees; one out of three had advanced degrees; only 3.8 percent had no college education at all. Those in scientific and engineering occupations had a significantly higher level of education:

	SCIENTISTS AND ENGINEERS (N = 214)	OTHER OCCUPATIONS (N = 341)	TOTAL (N = 555)
No college at all	0.9%	5.5%	3.8%
Bachelor's degree or more	92.6	77.0	83.0
Advanced degree	43.3	26.7	33.1

Doctorates had been earned by 22 percent of the scientific and engineering group and by 9.1 percent of the others. Level of education for both present and former employees is shown in more detail in Appendix D.

The 83 percent of college graduates compares with 78 percent of the Warner–Van Riper sample.[12] Civil Service Commission data on members of the Career Executive Roster show 72 percent with college degrees.[13]

EDUCATIONAL FIELDS. The employees and former employees were educated in a wide variety of fields:

---

[12] Warner *et al.*, *op. cit.*, p. 354.
[13] Bolster, *op. cit.*, p. 7.

	PERCENTAGE OF THOSE FOR WHOM COLLEGE MAJORS WERE REPORTED (N = 462)
Engineering	24.0%
Law	21.9
Social Sciences	14.1
Physical Sciences	13.4
Business and Commerce (including Accounting)	8.4
Mathematics and Statistics	3.5
Agriculture	3.5
Biological Sciences (including Medicine)	3.2
Education	3.0
English and Journalism	1.5
All other	3.5
	100.0

A tabulation relating fields of college study to occupations showed a natural tendency for the men to work in the fields in which they were educated. Of those in engineering work, 83.5 percent had majored in engineering; 64.4 percent of those in the physical sciences, mathematics, and statistics area had majored in science, and 12.3 percent in mathematics or statistics. Of those in general administration, more had studied law than any other field (19.4 percent).

Mobility

Employee mobility was analyzed by occupation, organization, and geography. In all these respects the higher civil servants tended to "stay put."

Occupational Mobility

An analysis of "number of different major occupational fields" [14] of present and former employees is shown on the following page:

[14] This term was used to describe common professional and administrative occupations in federal service—e.g., biology, law, engineering, budget, and procurement.

NUMBER OF MAJOR OCCUPATIONAL FIELDS	(N = 559)
One	56.5%
Two	27.7
Three	12.7
Four	2.7
Five	0.4
	100.0

There were no significant variations in this pattern when tabulations were made by departmental groupings or by period of entry into federal service.

Real occupational mobility was lower than the reader might infer from the foregoing table because many of the shifts shown were among closely related occupational fields—for example, from budget to general administration, or from engineering to physical sciences, mathematics, and statistics. Some of the numbers above "one" also result from difficulties in coding the data.

Shifts from "program" to "administrative" [15] occupational fields and vice versa were counted. About 19 percent of the group moved *into* one of the "administrative" occupations during his career. Of those who entered federal service before 1941, 29 percent made such moves. Only 8 percent of the total group studied moved *out* of the "administrative" fields.

A similar degree (or lack) of occupational mobility was also reported in the Corson study, where 69 percent of the respondents reported that all their jobs were in the same occupational group. Civil Service Commission figures also show very limited occupational mobility: "The chances are three to one that an executive's present position is in the same occupational area as his last position—or even the one before that." [16]

These results are generally consistent with those in a study of scientists' mobility made by the Bureau of Labor Statistics. Only one out of four of the 50,000 scientists covered had worked in more than one discipline in the course of his career.[17]

[15] Budget, finance, personnel, general administration, and management of resources.

[16] Bolster, *op. cit.*, p. 7.

[17] U. S. Department of Labor, Bureau of Labor Statistics, *Occupational Mobility of Scientists: A Study of Chemists, Biologists, and Physicists with Ph.D. Degrees*, Bulletin No. 1121 (February 1953).

In summary, then, higher civil servants are likely to stay in the same occupational fields. The most frequent kind of occupational movement is from a program field to an administrative field.

Organizational and Geographic Mobility

NUMBER OF ORGANIZATIONS. Over half of the group studied had worked in only one department or agency. About 30 percent had worked in only two. Movement among bureaus [18] within departments was also limited: 37 percent had worked in one bureau; 31 percent in two bureaus; and 17 percent in three.

Data from the present study show somewhat less mobility than the Corson study and much less than the Warner–Van Riper study (see Table 3.2).

TABLE 3.2. *Number of Departments, Bureaus, or Organizations in Which Employees Worked*
(Percentages according to number of organizations)

Number of Organizations	BROOKINGS STUDY		CORSON STUDY	WARNER–VAN RIPER STUDY
	Number of "Departments" (N = 559)	Number of "Bureaus" (N = 559)	Number of "Departments or Bureaus" (N = 424)	Number of "Organizations"[a] (N = 10,851)
One	55.8%	37.4%	38%	13%
Two	30.4	30.8	30	15
Three	9.3	17.5	18	17
Four	3.2	10.5	10	15
Five	0.9	2.9	3	12
Six	0.4	0.9	1	9
Seven	—	—	—	19
	100.0	100.0	100	100

[a] Warner *et al., op. cit.,* p. 170. Figures are for "career civil service executives." The much higher mobility shown by the Warner–Van Riper figures may be the result of respondents' interpretations of questionnaire instructions. The source data of this (Brookings) study were severely edited to eliminate cases in which units were moved from one agency to another. Our figures may also understate mobility because of the "every five years" technique used. This is a negligible factor, however, because an employee who has spent 15 or 20 years in one agency is unlikely to have left it and returned within 5 years.

[18] The term "bureau" means first major organizational level within a department or independent agency, regardless of its actual nomenclature.

MOVES BETWEEN HEADQUARTERS AND FIELD. A quarter of the group studied had transferred from the field to headquarters at some point in their careers. Fewer than half that number had moved in the opposite direction:

NUMBER OF SHIFTS	(N = 559) FROM FIELD TO HEADQUARTERS	FROM HEADQUARTERS TO FIELD
None	73.9%	88.2%
One	25.0	11.3
Two	1.1	.5

Leaving and Re-Entering Federal Service

Nearly all the career records (87.7 percent) showed continuous federal service. Nine percent had one gap in federal service. About 3 percent had two or more gaps in service.

Advancement

The typical higher federal employee, as noted at the beginning of this chapter, advanced six or seven grades in 20 years. More detail about patterns of advancement may be of interest.

Grade of First Job Shown

The federal careers of the group studied began at various levels. Apart from some concentration at the very bottom, their first jobs were spaced fairly evenly through the hierarchy of grades (see Table 3.3).

Total Grades Advanced

The number of grades by which higher civil servants advanced from the first position shown to the highest grade varied from zero to sixteen (see Table 3.4). The length of time needed to advance a given number of grades obviously varied from person to person.

TABLE 3.3. *Grades of Earliest Federal Job Shown on Career History Information Forms*

Earliest Job [a]	Present Employees (N = 344)	Former Employees (N = 166)	Total (N = 510)
Under GS-5	18.0%	16.3%	17.4%
GS-5	10.2	7.8	9.4
GS-6	1.5	.6	1.2
GS-7	11.6	8.4	10.6
GS-8	.3	.6	.4
GS-9	12.2	10.9	11.8
GS-10	.9	.6	.8
GS-11	8.7	12.7	10.0
GS-12	12.2	7.8	10.8
GS-13	7.8	10.8	8.8
GS-14	7.5	7.2	7.4
GS-15	6.4	13.9	8.8
GS-16 and above	2.7	2.4	2.6
	100.0	100.0	100.0
Median Grade	9	11	9

[a] Grades from other grading schedules—TVA, Foreign Service, Post Office, Executive Order (EO), Professional (P), Subprofessional (SP), Custodial (Cu), Crafts, Protective, and Custodial (CPC)—were converted to General Schedule (GS) or Clerical, Administrative, and Fiscal (CAF) equivalents.

Age and Length of Service To Reach Top Grade

The average member of the whole group studied was 49.2 years old when he first reached the highest grade shown.[19] The average present employee was 48 years old; the average former employee 51.5.

Employees of non-Defense Cabinet departments reached their top grades at a significantly older age (52 years) than those of Defense (47.2) or other agencies (48.2). Members of the scientific and engineering group also "got there younger" (47.4) than others (50.5).

The ages at which members of the group reached their top grades are shown on the following page:

[19] Averages cited in this section are arithmetic means.

AGE AT WHICH HIGHEST GRADE

REACHED IS FIRST SHOWN	(N = 556)
Under 25	—
25–29	0.3%
30–34	2.1
35–39	10.1
40–44	18.9
45–49	23.2
50–54	18.0
55–59	14.6
60–64	8.1
65–69	3.8
70 and over	0.9
	100.0

The top grades are reached after 20 years of federal service on the average. (Present employees, 20.1 years; former employees, 19.4.) As one would expect from the age data in the foregoing table, it took longer for an employee to reach his highest grade in a non-Defense department (22.1 years) than in the Department of Defense (17.8) or in other agencies (19.4). The scientific and engineering personnel reached their highest grades with less federal service (17.7 years) than others (21.3).

A distribution of the total sample follows:

YEARS OF FEDERAL SERVICE AT	
WHICH TOP GRADE IS REACHED	(N = 537)
Under 5	5.2%
5–9	7.6
10–14	14.5
15–19	20.5
20–24	21.8
25–29	17.0
30–34	6.5
35 and over	6.9
	100.0

TABLE 3.4. *Number of Grades Advanced by Present and Former Employees from First to Highest Positions Shown on Career History Information Forms*

Number of Grades Advanced	(N = 503)
0	10.3%
1	5.4
2	6.6
3	10.3
4	8.9
5	4.0
6	8.7
7	4.8
8	9.3
9	3.6
10	7.3
11	4.2
12	2.8
13	6.0
14	3.4
15	1.8
16	1.2
To "Other"	1.4
	100.0

Median: 6 grades

Rate of Advancement

The average civil servant advanced 6.3 grades in 20 years, or *about one grade every 3 years*. This rough average prevails regardless of major departmental or occupational categories.

There was a clear tendency, as one would expect, for these employees to advance more rapidly in the early stages of their careers. In general, they went up *three* grades from the first job shown to the second, five years later.[20] From the second to the third five-year period, they advanced *two* grades. After that they tended to advance *one* grade every five years.

Average advancement by five-year periods proceeded as follows:

POSITIONS ADVANCED	*N*	AVERAGE NUMBER OF GRADES ADVANCED
First to second	424	2.9
Second to third	395	2.0
Third to fourth	336	1.4
Fourth to fifth	252	1.2
Fifth to sixth	171	1.2
Sixth to seventh	84	1.1
Seventh to eighth	33	1.2

This pattern did not change significantly when analyzed by major departmental or occupational groupings.

In summary, then, career advancement by grades for the group studied was significant and steady, with more rapid progression near the start of the employee's career.

Conclusion

Sketched in the foregoing pages is the picture of a middle-aged group of professionals and managers who have spent most of their careers in the same occupational and organizational areas in the federal service. They have been steadily promoted over a 20-year period to their present high levels, or the levels from which they left the service. Few of them had short-term careers, meteoric rises, or service in many agencies. Of the employees who are still in federal service, a majority are eligible to retire in 5 to 10 years, and about half plan to do so.

[20] The career history data showed the jobs held by employees at five-year intervals. See Appendix A for fuller explanation.

4

Management Views of Federal Personnel Systems

INTERVIEWS WITH HIGH OFFICIALS of depart-
ments and agencies brought out advantages and disadvantages, not
only of the civil service system but also of other federal personnel
systems.

Views on the Higher Civil Service

Management officials in the federal government view the higher
civil service with a mixture of satisfaction and discontent. All of those
whose judgments are reflected in this study strongly praised the skill
and dedication of the higher employees. Roughly half of those interviewed think "we're doing about as well as we can." The others have
a variety of negative comments and positive suggestions.

Most of the judgments reported come from interviews with 67
officials in high management positions in departments and agencies.[1]
The group included both political executives and career executives, in
a ratio of about one of the former to two of the latter. Responses of
political executives and of career executives did not differ significantly.

Although the interviews followed a standard outline the officials

[1] The remainder of the 100 management interviews referred to in Appendix A
were less formally organized and recorded.

expressed themselves freely. Generalizations drawn from these replies have to be attempted, but they fail to do justice to the intensity, ingenuity, and cogency of many of the individual answers.

It must also be recognized that a bias favorable to the *status quo* runs through these interviews. As one adviser put it, ". . . the members of a system, especially those who have won their way to its top ranks, can hardly judge either its present or future viability except in terms which acknowledge the system's virtues in choosing them as its leaders."

Qualities Needed

The interviewees were asked what factors contributed to the success of employees they regarded as outstanding. In their replies they gave overwhelming emphasis to such mental qualities as analytical keenness, depth of judgment, and imagination. The qualities mentioned next most often were sound technical experience and training for the work to be done, and energy, drive, and willingness to work hard and long. These were followed by ability to communicate and to work well with others and by dedication to public service.

They were also asked about factors that caused unsatisfactory or mediocre job performance. The two most frequently mentioned were inability to get along with others and insufficient technical competence.

Forecasting Needs and Taking Inventory

Interviewers asked management officials: "Have you been able to install a satisfactory system for forecasting your future needs for personnel at these levels and for analyzing how able the organization is to meet these needs?"

Of those who answered this question, more than 40 percent frankly said that their agencies have no system, or no satisfactory system, for doing this. Some of these said that they simply assumed that their present needs would continue. This is a disturbingly high negative response, considering the turnover that can be anticipated and the extent to which higher federal jobs have been filled from within (as shown in Chapter 3).

The replies of those who answered affirmatively tended to overlap with their answers to the next question asked: "How do you try to identify employees of outstanding potential for top career jobs? How early in their careers is this done? What is done to keep track of, or develop, people so identified?"

Some merely indicated that they were keeping track of retirement eligibility of key employees and were informally identifying and evaluating understudies.

The exceptional interviewees were those who reported tangible measures to estimate the number and characteristics of top personnel needed in the future and to find out how ready their present employees are to meet these future needs. The Veterans Administration maintains a five-year forecast of needs for key personnel, and runs an inventory and appraisal program in which potential replacements are evaluated in depth. In the Department of Labor officials of the Bureau of Labor Statistics and the Bureau of Employment Security reported keeping tables of future requirements. The Department of the Navy maintains a central registry of all departmental employees at and above GS–11. These employees are interviewed periodically about their qualifications and interests. The Bureau of the Budget evaluates all professional staff semiannually for placement and development purposes. Both the Department of Agriculture and the Federal Aviation Agency are preparing to put personnel inventory records on automatic data processing equipment. The FAA requires supervisors to list employees as "ready replacements" or "potential replacements" for top positions, and an executive personnel board controls development of personnel for such positions. The Department of Commerce requires each bureau to rate its ten most outstanding employees in each occupational field; these lists are then reviewed centrally and "boiled down" as a basis for referrals and placements.

Other agencies reporting success in career planning for top personnel included the Social Security Administration, the Internal Revenue Service, the Patent Office, and the Department of the Air Force.

The relatively loose interview pattern used in the present study did not furnish data for a complete agency-by-agency evaluation of executive forecasting and inventory programs. It is clear, however, that the federal service in general is deficient in procedures for assessing future needs and the material to meet them. This judgment agrees with that of the Chief of the Civil Service Commission's Bureau of Inspections and Classification Audits, who spoke of "a real lack of total managerial planning for basic manpower needs."

Filling and Preparing To Fill Civil Service Jobs

PROBLEMS IN GENERAL. "What problems have you had in filling jobs in GS–15 through 18 (or in keeping them filled) with top quality people?

More than 40 percent of the management representatives surprised their interviewers by answering, in effect, "few" or "none." They reported that top level jobs were filled with people of competence and dedication, that turnover was low, and that "back-up" was adequate. Some said this situation resulted from such factors as the interesting mission of the agency, or the good reputation of its chief. Others (e.g., Navy, Social Security, Bureau of the Budget) said they were now benefiting from large numbers of able young employees appointed in previous years.

The 60 percent who reported problems in filling higher civil service jobs mentioned salary difficulties more than any other topic. Most frequently they said that federal pay levels were not competitive with private industry. They commented also on problems resulting from quota limitations on "supergrade" positions and "rigidities" in classification. About an equal number said that some jobs were very hard to fill because they were in shortage occupations or because they had unusual or difficult requirements.

A wide variety of other problems were mentioned: inability to pay moving expenses, inability of the personnel system to "produce" qualified people, slow personnel processing, the relative unattractiveness of the agency's program, conflict of interest rules, and "political overtones."

A typical comment was made by one eminent agency head:

I had much less success than I had expected in bringing people into this agency from the outside. The two major problems have been salary limitations and delay, including the delay in getting security clearances, which has often been irksome.

WHERE DO PEOPLE COME FROM TO FILL TOP JOBS? Asked about sources from which able top personnel were obtained, interviewees replied in these ways:

	PERCENTAGE NAMING A SOURCE [2] (N = 64)
From inside the agency or department	64%
From outside the government	48
From other agencies in the government	39
From inside the division (or other work unit)	28

The commonest pattern was to try to fill jobs first from within the agency, then from other agencies, then from outside the government.

To a question on the Civil Service Commission's Career Executive Roster,[3] civil service registers, and other facilities, 45 percent said they did not make use of any of the three; 29 percent had considered referrals from the Career Executive Roster; 18 percent had used registers; 10 percent had used other facilities; some had used more than one of them. Many of those who had used the Roster and registers questioned their value.

HOW WELL "BACKED UP" ARE HIGHER JOBS? Management officials were asked: "How well backed up are jobs in these levels? (That is, are there able people in the organization available to step up—people with enough breadth of knowledge and experience?)"

Their answers (simplified, of course):

	(N = 60)
Very well	38%
Poorly or not as well as they should be	35
Pretty well	10
Well for some specialized jobs; poorly for others	7
Other comments	10

Some of the officials gave "it depends" answers, such as:

Well "backed up" at GS–15 and 16, but not at 17 and 18
People appointed in the 1930's are more able than those appointed later
Better "backed up" in numbers than in quality.

[2] Percentages add to more than 100 because many interviewees said they used two or more sources.
[3] A list of "supergrade" employees, used for job referrals.

On the basis of these replies one could hardly characterize federal management as well satisfied in this important matter.

Said the head of one large agency:

> I would say that the jobs in these levels are well backed up. We regard it as a part of a manager's job to develop successors. We constantly watch all of the key posts to make sure that we have someone in line as a successor, and the managers who do the best job of developing their successors are rewarded, with the result that any who overlook this essential part of their jobs quickly become conspicuous and we call their oversight to their attention.

Another was dissatisfied. According to the interview report:

> He is very unhappy with his "back-up" situation. This goes back to the period of about 1955 and 1956 when there was a big increase beginning in [agency] responsibilities, but no corresponding increase in the number of personnel. This means that experienced people have been spread very thin, and he thinks the needs of the future will have to be met by bringing in outside talent.

Also dissatisfied was a high departmental official, but for a different reason:

> Very poorly backed up. The big problem, according to Mr. ———, is the need for people with good analytical minds who can thoughtfully and logically analyze a problem and then synthesize solutions. They have to be able and prompt in their decisions and must be able to write concise, clear English. Breadth of experience and viewpoint is also important.

Moving and Developing Higher Civil Service Employees

MOVING THEM TO MEET PROGRAM NEEDS. About two-thirds of the management officials answered "No" to the question: "Have you had any problems in assigning, transferring, or borrowing people at these levels to meet urgent program needs?" (The low mobility figures in Chapter 3 suggest that such officials may not have tried to move employees much.) Those who answered affirmatively were concerned about disruptive effects on either the work to be done or on the employees concerned.

FURTHER DEVELOPMENT OF TOP PERSONNEL. No systematic survey of executive training and development activities was attempted, but the management interviewees were asked: "What is being done (in an organized way) to develop further the skills and understanding of people in these top four grades?" Some of these officials were (significantly) unfamiliar with the details of such activities. Replies of those who answered this question can be summarized as follows: [4]

	(N = 48)
In-service seminars, programs, and courses (within own agency)	50%
Outside short-term courses, seminars, conferences	44
Other seminars and courses within the government	25
Graduate school attendance (9 months and more)	23
Do little or nothing	19
Attendance at professional meetings	15
Rotation among jobs	2

(Fourteen respondents mentioned one of the above types of activities; 12 mentioned two; and 12, three.)

There were a significant number of informal observations about the need for members of the higher civil service to be trained further in concepts and skills of good management.

Losing Higher Civil Service Employees

Asked why able employees in grades GS–15 through 18 leave the federal service, 60 percent of the management officials said "for more money," or words to that effect. Thirty-one percent said "Few leave"; of these, 12 percent said "Few leave, but those who do, leave for more money." A large group (47 percent) mentioned nonfinancial reasons for other jobs being more attractive: better advancement prospects, desire to teach, desire to move to private industry. Other reasons were miscellaneous. Only a few officials mentioned "politics," office space and parking, exposure to difficult pressures, and personal reasons.

When the management officials were asked at what levels higher civil services employees were most likely to leave, 33 percent said "below GS–15," 31 percent said "at GS–15," and other replies were scattered or inconclusive.

[4] Percentages add to more than 100 because several methods were named by some respondents.

Interviewees were asked to name outstanding higher employees who had left federal service and to tell who employed them. The present employers of these former civil servants include large industries, prominent law firms, consulting firms, leading universities, and trade associations.

What To Do About the Mediocre?

"What is done (and can be done) in the case of people at these levels whose job performance is mediocre or unsatisfactory?"

Answers to this question can be grouped under a few main categories: [5]

	(N = 59)
Reassign them	51%
Force them out (including discharge for cause)	36
Nothing can be done; or, this is very difficult	24
Put pressure on them to retire	15
Abolish their jobs	15
Counsel them	10
Give further training	8

These responses are difficult to interpret and evaluate. There may, in fact, be very few mediocre or unsatisfactory employees in the top grades. Where they exist, some management officials may not acknowledge the problem. For whatever reason, about a quarter of the interviewees began their answers by saying, "We rarely [or never] have a mediocre employee at this level."

The fact that there *is* a problem is suggested by the fact that one out of four said in effect, "nothing can be done," and that one out of two said, "reassign them"—which in many cases would just change the locale of the difficulty. The "nothing can be done" responses were of two main types: (1) It is simply too hard to make a case against a long-service employee whose only problem is that he isn't competent enough. (2) Some mediocre employees have connections with influential persons. Said one assistant secretary:

So far as the category "mediocre" is concerned, this is an unsolved problem in the permanent civil service: how to prove that, if he has

[5] Percentages add to more than 100 because of multiple answers.

not been fired in 35 years on the job, he is mediocre. Adding to the difficulty is the fact that the general public does not understand the problem. I have been watching this since February 1937. Professional personnel management people say the system of discharge works perfectly, but according to my observation it does not.

Changes Desired by Management

The key question in the management interviews was: "What changes would you like to see made in how personnel matters are handled for top federal employees?" Some of the officials felt unprepared to answer and said that they wished the question had been given them in advance. Such advance preparation, however, probably would have involved staff help by others. It was considered more desirable to seek each management official's immediate personal reaction. Since the question came near the end of the interview, the respondent was stimulated and at least partly prepared by discussion of the preceding questions.

A majority of the group expressed general satisfaction with the present situation. Nearly all, satisfied or otherwise, had some suggestions for improvement. Answers were "all over the map," but the most frequent recommendations can be categorized.

CLASSIFICATION AND SALARIES. The most frequent changes suggested under this heading were higher salaries and classification practices more closely conforming to management's needs. Thirty-six percent of the interviewees asked that salaries be raised or "made competitive." They and others also made suggestions about classification:

	(N = 64)
Adopt a "rank in man" or "earned status" plan [6]	23%
Remove numerical limits on "supergrades" (GS-16, 17, and 18)	16
Abandon "supergrade" classification and handle salaries like those under P.L. 313 (i.e., without grading)	14
Let agencies decide their own "supergrade" allocations	9

MOBILITY. Another recurring class of ideas concerned more movement of employees among agencies and locations. Some interviewees said

[6] See Chapter 6 for discussion.

that more mobility should be forced; others, that it should be encouraged.

DISMISSALS. There were 13 proposals to simplify dismissal procedures or to permit agencies to force out employees at higher levels without formal proceedings.

OTHER IDEAS. The remaining suggestions were more scattered. They referred to a number of topics already discussed earlier in the interviews. These are listed in order of frequency:

Speed up appointments and clearances
Establish more effective recruitment programs
Step up higher level training activities; establish a civilian staff college
Provide more stringent and accurate methods for evaluating employees
Achieve stronger personnel program leadership by top management
Reduce or eliminate political interference
Repeal veterans' preference

Summary

Management officials, although reasonably well satisfied with their ability to attract and keep competent employees in the top four grades, see the need for improvement. They particularly note the desirability of better forecasting and planning systems and favor more liberal salaries and more flexible classification.

Views on Other Federal Personnel Systems

It was not possible within the time and resources available for this study to make a thoroughgoing review of other personnel systems in the federal service comparable with the higher civil service. It was possible, however, to make use of information and judgments about the military officer personnel system, the Commissioned Corps system of the Public Health Service, and the Foreign Service personnel system.[7]

The corps systems differ considerably from the regular civil service in important respects. They place greater emphasis on initial selection at bottom levels. They base compensation on rank held rather than on evaluation of the duties performed. Selection for promotion is administered on a corps-wide basis, rather than job by job. Relatively early retirement is made possible; or, in the case of the military systems, required in order to provide advancement opportunities for younger officers. The officer regards his primary affiliation as being with the corps, rather than with a specific job, and has a sense of pride in his membership in the corps. Perhaps most important of all, responsibility for the development, assignment, and best use of the officers belongs to the corps itself—or to those who manage its personnel operations. In the civil service, by contrast, such responsibility is diffused among many layers of program executives and staff personnel offices—to say nothing of control responsibilities retained by the Civil Service Commission.

When these other systems are compared with the elements of a model personnel system postulated in Chapter 2, they seem to be superior to the civil service system in some respects and less satisfactory in others.

Needs of the Future

Both the Foreign Service and the Commissioned Corps of the Public Health Service could greatly improve their ability to forecast future

[7] Sources include three interviews with personnel officials of the Foreign Service, six interviews with officers or former officers of the military personnel systems, and one interview with a former official of the Department of Medicine and Surgery of the Veterans Administration. Some information about these systems was also included in 22 of the management interviews with officials whose jurisdiction covered commissioned personnel as well as civil service personnel. As noted in Chapter 2, several reports of studies of these other systems were reviewed. Additional sources included group meetings attended by persons familiar with their personnel systems, and the author's personal knowledge, based on nine years' working experience with military officers and with the Commissioned Corps of the Public Health Service.

The judgments presented are not statistically supported, but they are fairly representative comments made on the subjects under consideration.

manpower needs. This is clearly brought out both in the Herter Committee Report [8] and in the Folsom Committee Report.[9]

Interview data brought out the fact that both the Foreign Service and the Commissioned Corps of the Public Health Service are in only the early stages of taking action on corrective recommendations. The military personnel systems, however, have for years emphasized advance planning of manpower needs based on assigned missions; such planning is reflected in tables of organization.

All three types of systems maintain centralized records, so that inventories of personnel qualifications are available.

Competition for Professionals and Executives

Recruitment was not specifically discussed with representatives of the military services, but interviews indicated some concern with the lack of attractiveness of military pay (until the increases of autumn 1963) in comparison with civil service salaries as well as with salaries outside the government. The Herter and Folsom reports frankly faced the fact that the Foreign Service and the Public Health Service are not attracting the best quality people in college graduating classes. The Herter Report recommended recruitment at Classes 7 and 6 of the Foreign Service instead of Class 8 in order to meet competition. It also recommended greater emphasis on recruiting at intermediate and higher levels. The Folsom Report frankly stated that the civil service system "provides flexibilities in appointing at senior levels which the commissioned corps does not." [10]

Evaluating Performance and Potential

Those who were interviewed generally referred to the difficult human problems involved in obtaining accurate evaluations of officers' performance and potential. In the military services there has been a

[8] *Personnel for the New Diplomacy: Report of the Committee on Foreign Affairs Personnel* (Carnegie Endowment for International Peace, December 1962), p. 63.

[9] *Report of the Advisory Committee on Public Health Service Personnel Systems* (U.S. Department of Health, Education, and Welfare, March 1962), p. 7.

[10] *Ibid.*, p. 2.

tendency for the evaluations in performance reports to rise gradually until officers of only moderate capacities are rated in a next-to-top category. This tendency has been met by repeated revisions of performance report methods and forms in order to force specific judgments and to reduce the "halo effect." In the Foreign Service considerable satisfaction was expressed with the system of narrative performance reports, which are made on change of supervision and at periodic intervals. The Herter Committee Report, however, recommended a much more rigorous evaluation of performance of people who are being considered for promotion from Class 3 to Class 2.

Training and Development

Military personnel systems devote major emphasis in an officer's career on his professional development. A few interviewees indicated that as much as one-third of a military officer's time was spent in formal schooling of one kind or another. A lower estimate appears in a work on this subject which stated that an officer who attains general's or admiral's rank has probably spent a total of at least two, and possibly three, years in advanced education—equivalent to the postgraduate work required in most professions.[11] This is not inconsistent with the Herter Committee's comparison of training time for four types of federal personnel. The Committee estimated the proportion of officers' training time to their total time as follows (figures exclude language training):[12]

U.S. Information Agency Reserve Officers	Slightly over 2 percent
Agency for International Development (including participating agency personnel)	Slightly over 2 percent
Foreign Service (and Reserve) Officers	About 5 percent
Military departments	Roughly 12 percent

Military officers are deliberately assigned to billets in order to give them overseas experience, command experience, and varieties of technical experience suited to their individual specialties. In some

[11] John W. Masland and Laurence I. Radway, *Soldiers and Scholars* (Princeton University Press, 1957), p. 73.
[12] *Personnel for the New Diplomacy, op. cit.*, p. 105.

cases they are given extensive periods of assignment to educational institutions; and other outside sources of instruction are used. One officer, for example, was reported to have spent a year at the Council on Foreign Relations in New York and after that two years at the Massachusetts Institute of Technology. In general, interviewees believed that officers are selected for education in the correct numbers and with the correct qualifications. A minority, however, stated that the assignment process is too mechanistic and that the object seems to be "to fill training slots" rather than to get the men developed.

Despite the recognized successes of the Foreign Service Institute and the long experience of developing Foreign Service Officers through a variety of assignments, the Herter Committee recommended more emphasis on training and development, including individually designed career development programs for officers; interchange among the Department of State, the Agency for International Development and the U.S. Information Agency; and the establishment of a national Foreign Affairs College. The Committee also recommended that the training programs be given at appropriate stages in the officers' careers.

The Folsom Committee Report on the Public Health Service noted a need for establishing career development programs on a more systematic basis.

Selection

Interviews concerning military personnel promotion systems resulted in general agreement that selection boards were a necessity because of their independence and objectivity. This was also true in discussion of the Foreign Service system. Interviewees recognized that such boards may make two kinds of mistakes: promoting some officers who should not be promoted, and passing over outstanding officers who should be. A minority of those interviewed indicated that "personal politics" sometimes influences selection boards and that personal lobbying and agreements among an "in" group have a considerable influence on selection decisions. Virtually every discussion of this topic ended with the conclusion that there were many things wrong with the system, but that no superior alternative had been devised. The interviewees found use of military selection boards clearly preferable to the more subjective, individualized approach characteristic of many selections in the higher civil service. The interviewees' suggestions for improvement dealt mainly with changes in the time required for eligibility for promotion or in the percentages of officers eligible.

The Herter Committee Report on the Foreign Service indicates a need for more rigorous review and evaluation of the qualifications and abilities of individuals, particularly before they are selected into the midcareer level (Foreign Service Class 5) and into the top level (Foreign Service Class 2).

Discussion of the Public Health Service Commissioned Corps personnel selection system was characterized by criticism of its unsystematic nature. The Folsom Report mentions selection of people whose backgrounds are poorly adapted to the jobs to be filled.

Opportunity To Advance

Military personnel systems have more limited opportunities for promotion as ranks become higher. The percentages of officers who can be promoted to the various ranks are stated in law. These restrictions result in attrition of officers who are not selected for promotion or who feel they are not going to be selected for promotion.

There are also limitations in the number of opportunities available for promotion of Public Health Service officers and Foreign Service officers, but the interviews revealed no adverse comment.

Movement To Meet Program Needs

Flexibility of assignment, both for developmental purposes and for purposes of meeting program needs, is characteristic of commissioned services. Unlike the higher civil servant, the military officer or Foreign Service officer or Public Health Service officer is affiliated with the corps of which he is a member rather than with a particular job, and he may be assigned to another type of duty, to another geographical location, or to an educational institution without loss of tenure, status, or salary. This has resulted in a high degree of mobility among military officers and Foreign Service officers. This is less true of the Public Health Service Commissioned Corps, where some officers have been at the same location, or have even been performing the same duties, for more than a decade.

Flexibility of movement in these corps systems is facilitated by a central set of records and a central personnel assignment staff.

Salary Levels

Interviewees said that salary increases were essential if the services were to compete successfully for needed personnel. The military services did receive increases in the fall of 1963, amounting to a raise of about 10 percent in base pay at the level of colonel/captain and about 5 percent in base pay of brigadier general/rear admiral. This was the first increase in basic pay for the military establishment since 1958. Commissioned officers of the Public Health Service were benefited by the same legislation. Foreign Service salaries were raised in the fall of 1962, and again in the summer of 1964.

Retention and Utilization

The forced attrition and the relatively early retirement of some military officers tends to result in the loss of competent personnel with many years of service ahead of them. Interviewees did not question this policy because it was considered necessary to make room for up-and-coming officers, but they agreed that it posed serious problems. In the Foreign Service there is a similar provision, which permits officers to be eliminated if they have served over a certain length of time in their particular classes. The Herter Committee noted that this provision has been used little and recommended its rescission.

In the Public Health Service, officers may apply for voluntary retirement after 20 years of service. Interviewees said that this provision has resulted in premature loss of some outstanding officers.

Motivation

There was general agreement among interviewees that personnel take special pride in being members of a military officer corps, the

Foreign Service, or the Commissioned Corps of the Public Health Service. This motivating factor goes beyond the pride in public service and pride in job reported for the higher civil service (see Chapter 5) and may be regarded as a major advantage of a corps system.

Mediocre or Unsatisfactory Employees

In interviews covering the corps services there was only a little discussion of problems of dealing with officers whose work is not up to standard. In the military services some such officers will fail of selection to higher rank and may then apply for retirement if they have the required service. Others are compulsorily retired if they are over age in grade or if they have completed 30 years of service. Actual selection-out measures for unsatisfactory service are rarely used.

It was strongly emphasized in the interviews that it is relatively easy in these managed corps systems to assign personnel to work that is of a level suited to their capacities. This can be done without endangering the rank, salary, or tenure of the individual and very often without labeling him as a failure.

At this writing the Department of State is considering strengthened selection-out measures for the Foreign Service.

Some further comparisons between these systems and the higher civil service appear in Chapters 6 and 7.

5

Employee Views of the Higher Civil Service

EMPLOYEES AND FORMER EMPLOYEES have furnished impressive testimony on the values of federal careers and some sharp insights into the deficiencies. The prevailing theme was one of satisfaction, but there were many thoughtful, strongly worded suggestions for improvement. The reader should remember that these judgments are expressed mainly by people who "have it made," and therefore tend to favor the systems that helped them get where they are. The viewpoints in this chapter are drawn from interviews of more than 150 employees, and from questionnaires completed by 103 present employees and 98 former employees.[1]

Factors in Employees' Careers

How They Got Their Jobs

The vast majority of the group studied were promoted or transferred to their present jobs as well as to the previous two jobs.

In both interviews and questionnaires the question was asked, "How did you get your present job?" A majority indicated that they were

[1] These are different persons from the respondents whose views are presented in Chapter 4. See Appendix A for explanation of survey and sampling methods.

selected because higher officials knew them or had observed their work. Some examples:

Cabinet department lawyer: I was recommended to the General Counsel . . . by a mutual friend in the private practice of law.

A top executive of an independent agency: Promotion from within. This was a new job at the time I took it over and I was requested to take it by the Executive Director.

Economist in a Cabinet department: My present chief was looking for a right-hand man to head up his operations research staff. A former colleague of mine recommended me to him, when the opening came to his attention. I was called, I expressed interest, I was interviewed, and finally selected.

Statistician in a Cabinet department: I was assigned by the Secretary of the Department from another position in the Secretary's office. I have been a member of the career staff in this Department since 1938. I have been assigned to a succession of positions by Departmental officials, on their motion.

This personal acquaintanceship factor probably was present in the case of many others who simply reported "by promotion" or "by transfer."

Tempted to Leave?

Asked if they had been approached about jobs in other agencies, 60 percent of those who replied said "Yes," and 40 percent, "No." The percentage of scientists and engineers who had been so approached was slightly below that of employees in other occupations. Those employees who had had such "nibbles" indicated that they resulted from professional and personal acquaintance.

In the personal interviews, employees were asked if they had been approached about jobs outside the federal government. The results were 71 percent "Yes" and 29 percent "No." More scientists and engineers reported such approaches (84 percent) than others (62 percent).

A typical comment was made by a data processing specialist in a large agency:

Yes. I've received offers from life insurance companies, and recently I had an offer from a state agency at $25,000 a year, which I found a little difficulty in turning down, but due to the satisfaction with my present work here I passed it up.

What Helped or Hindered Their Careers

The higher civil servants were invited to comment, both in interviews and questionnaires, on factors that had helped or hindered their careers. The types of factors most frequently mentioned as *helpful* were:

	(N = 352)
Education and training	45%
Opportunities; challenge	43
Experience	32
Competence; ability	28
Good supervision	21
Luck	21
Hard work	19

Asked what factors tended to *hinder* their careers, 37 percent serenely replied "None," or words to that effect. Other replies were so scattered as to be insignificant, but included partisan politics, poor supervision, the employee's own personality traits, lack of opportunity, and lack of education.

THE CIVIL SERVICE COMMISSION. Employees who received questionnaires were asked: "Have actions of the Civil Service Commission ever helped or hindered your career? What were they? How did they do this?" Results:

	(N = 100)
Made no difference	71%
Helped	17
Hindered	9
Some help; some hindrance	3
	——
	100

Specific "helps" mentioned included upgrading jobs and aid in acquiring career status. "Hindrances" were usually delays imposed by classification procedures or qualification requirements.

The main point, of course, is that the employees do not see any direct effect of Civil Service Commission actions on their careers. It would be natural to expect this, in view of delegations of personnel authority to the departments and agencies.

In general the higher civil servants studied take a favorable view of opportunities for getting ahead. This is consistent with the findings of the Kilpatrick "federal image" study, which found that ". . . these high-level employees feel considerable satisfaction about the advancement opportunities in government. On the other hand, they still give the business corporation a slight advantage over the government as a route to 'real success' . . ."[2]

Training Courses

The questionnaire for present employees asked if the employee had taken formal training courses at government expense. A little under half answered in the affirmative. Most of the training mentioned consisted of short courses in general management, supervision, or personnel administration. A few reported technical courses related to their occupations. Almost all comments about this training were favorable.

Details to Other Jobs

The employee questionnaires also asked: "Were you ever detailed from one job to another for a significant period? If so, was this an aid or a hindrance to your career development?" Of the 99 who replied, 45 had been detailed, 54 had not. Thirty-eight out of the 45 commented; 34 (or 89 percent) called these assignments helpful.

Principal Attitudes Expressed

Higher federal employees are generally well satisfied with many factors in their careers, and they take pride in their work. They have a

[2] Franklin P. Kilpatrick, Milton C. Cummings, Jr., M. Kent Jennings, *The Image of the Federal Service* (Brookings Institution, 1964), p. 162. This book and its companion volume, *Source Book of a Study of Occupational Values and the Image of the Federal Service*, are cited at several points in this chapter. They contain extensive information about the views of federal executives, natural scientists, social scientists, and engineers. These studies also contain data on the judgments of the general employed public and of various groups with respect to their own occupational goals and to the federal government as an employer. They will be cited as *Image* and *Source Book*, respectively.

high regard for their agencies and their associates, but they are concerned about bureaucratic complexities and obstacles.

Satisfactions and Dissatisfactions

SATISFACTIONS. They mentioned many different things when invited to
state the main satisfactions of their careers, but the comments fell into
a few main categories, as shown in Table 5.1.

Other replies were scattered and difficult to categorize.

These figures cannot be analyzed closely. The semantic distinctions
are risky, and differences of a few points are not statistically significant.

It is clear, however, that the scientists and engineers place a higher
value on professional achievement and work freedom, while the others
take more satisfaction in public service in general. Both groups appear
strongly motivated by nonfinancial considerations and relatively little
concerned with job security.

The *Image* study also reported high ratings on what might be
called work values and relatively low ratings on factors concerned with
job security.[3]

Two excerpts from interview reports point up the main thoughts
expressed by many:

Defense official: Most of ———'s satisfactions with a federal
career can be rounded up under the heading of professional opportunities. For someone of his background and interests there have
been tremendous challenges and lots of room both to make a contribution and to get involved in solving a variety of problems and
having new experiences all around. He also derives satisfaction from
knowing that he is really on the frontiers of the most advanced
management practice. He compares this favorably with the rather
more remote academic life which he had originally intended to
pursue.

Program officer in a Cabinet department: My satisfactions have
been primarily the opportunity to deal with matters of great importance and the fact that responsibility has been delegated in such
manner that I've been free to go ahead and do a job. The fact too
that I feel that the business of government is important to our society
and the orderly disposition of problems is worth the effort and highly
satisfying.

[3] Kilpatrick, *et al., Source Book,* pp. 181–82.

TABLE 5.1. *Principal Career Satisfactions Named by Present and Former Employees in Interviews and Questionnaires*

Career Satisfactions	Scientific, Engineering, and Technical (N = 150)	Other (N = 202)	Total (N = 352)
Challenge, scope, variety of work	46%	39%	42%
Sense of accomplishment	46	36	41
Public service; sense of mission	24	44	36
Working with good associates	26	28	27
Pride in making a contribution	37	16	25
Freedom to work on one's own	25	8	16
Influencing important public policy	8	11	10
Developing employees	7	7	7
Prestige of government (or agency)	3	10	7
Job security	7	5	6

DISSATISFACTIONS. Invited to state their dissatisfactions, the group named such a scattered collection of problems and grievances that only a few points stand out clearly. The main points made are shown in Table 5.2.

Causes of dissatisfaction mentioned less frequently included—

Lack of resources or support for program
"Poor federal image"
Political interference and changes
Mediocre or incompetent associates
Lack of recognition for good work

TABLE 5.2. *Principal Career Dissatisfactions Named by Present and Former Employees in Interviews and Questionnaires*

Career Dissatisfactions	Scientific, Engineering, and Technical (N = 150)	Other (N = 202)	Total (N = 352)
"Government complexity"—slow procedures, multiple clearances, excessive paperwork, too many rules, duplication of effort, etc.	54%	39%	45%
Timid or otherwise inadequate supervision	19	18	18
Inadequate pay levels	11	16	13
"None"	9	13	11

Note that the scientists and engineers were significantly more concerned about "red tape" factors than the other employees, and significantly less concerned about salaries. The "red tape" factors seem consistent with Kilpatrick's finding that "lack of self-determination" is a negative job attribute.[4] The inadequate supervision factor also emerges as a "federal image" finding.[5]

A few quotations illustrate the "red tape," "timid supervision," and salary factors vividly:

Economist in a Cabinet department: The occasional lack of clear communication and direction, perhaps inevitable in such a large government system. The unnecessary time spent in budget-making because budgets are one-year and too many officials review them; the devastating effects on people and organization of drastic changes in staff and budget (e.g., the cut of 1947); the red tape and delay in making appointments; the inability to get rid of ineffective, mediocre performers without spending too much time on it; the "witch hunts" of the McCarthy era and their terrible effects on innocent individuals and on the image of government.

Executive administering grant-in-aid program: He gets very tired of paper shuffling, and such tasks as the preparation of agendas for field conferences. He is bored by administrative negotiations, and by the necessity of working with such matters as travel allotments, space allocations, and staffing. He is also troubled by the tendency of becoming anonymous in a large bureaucracy, and feels the need for more personal identification with important results. He feels that staff members who come from state agencies are particularly subject to such feelings of frustration. They have a tough time getting used to the necessity for clearing actions with so many specialists. After they do it for a while, "the heart seems to go out of them."

Former engineering executive in an independent agency: The ineffectiveness of some persons in highly placed positions of responsibility and the tendency of contemporaries to "go along" when the chips were down, rather than be heard.

Former program executive of a military department: The contrast between the salaries of competent executives in government and in business. It is ridiculous for example that in four years in private industry I will pay from taxes on my salary all the [amount] I earned in 21 years with the government although I was a supergrade for 8 of those years. . . . The array of controls in government that are

4 *Ibid.*, p. 205.
5 *Ibid.*, p. 201.

based on assumptions of personal lack of integrity were the most onerous things.

This comment from a better-satisfied executive is interesting:

> Program executive in a Cabinet department: This question surprises me. I had not thought of any [dissatisfactions]. As civil servants, naturally, we have some exasperations—we make recommendations and find that because of political considerations they are unacceptable. This is a continuous irritant, but as you mature you realize that there are two sides to this question. On the whole, I am not dissatisfied with anything.

Judgments on Use of Skills

Present employees were asked, "On the average, for what percent of your working time are you making good use of your professional knowledge?" This question was interpreted in various ways. Some gave low percentages if they were not using professional or technical skills (e.g., science, engineering, accounting) on the job. Others regarded such skills as a necessary background for their work and gave high percentages. Still others enlarged the definition of "skills" to include supervision and administration; they too reported high percentages.

Of the present employees reached by questionnaire or interview, results were as follows:

PERCENTAGE OF WORKING TIME MAKING GOOD USE OF PROFESSIONAL SKILLS	PERCENTAGE OF RESPONDENTS (N = 237)
100%	34%
90–100	18
75–90	25
Under 75	23
	——
	100

Most of them, therefore, are satisfied in this respect.

Judgments on the Agency and Top Career Officials

The present employees interviewed were asked: "What is your general judgment as to the effectiveness and competence of your organization in doing its job?"

	(N = 150)
Excellent, "terrific," outstanding, very good	53%
Good on the whole, pretty good	40
Part good, part poor	5
Poor	2
	100

On the questionnaires employees were asked to comment upon "the general professional competence and cooperativeness of persons in your occupational field in your department." Here the "report card" was even more favorable:

	(N = 101)
Excellent, very good	76%
Good on the whole	14
Part good, part poor	7
Poor	3
	100

Said two respondents:

Procurement official in a military department: Very good, terrific. We have an extremely competent organization both administratively and technically.

Executive of an independent agency: ——— has as highly dedicated a corps of people as it is possible to secure. The agency is very effective in getting its job done.

Each interviewee was also asked if he preferred to work for his department or agency above all others. Of the 144 who replied, 76 percent said Yes; 19 percent said that they liked their present situation but would be willing to go to another agency; and 5 percent indicated no real preference for their agencies.

Why They Stay—Why They Leave

Reasons for Staying in Federal Service

In order to focus attention on primary motivations, employees were asked, in both interviews and questionnaires, "Why do you stay in federal service?" The replies showed some clear and interesting patterns (see Table 5.3).

TABLE 5.3. *Leading Reasons for Staying in Federal Service Given by Present Employees in Interviews and Questionnaires*

Reasons for Staying	Scientific, Engineering, and Technical (N = 116)	Other (N = 146)	Total (N = 262)
Challenge, scope, variety, importance of work	59%	62%	61%
Stake in retirement system and other security factors	41	28	34
"Public service"	17	35	27
Working with good associates	21	16	18
Sense of achievement	18	12	15
Adequate pay	16	10	13
Inertia, reluctance to change	13	6	9

The scientists' and engineers' greater emphasis on retirement and less emphasis on "public service" are statistically significant, compared with the attitudes of the "other" group.

The emphasis on work values is consistent with the "career satisfactions" reported above. It is also consistent with the findings in the *Image* study.[6]

Typical comments were like these:

Scientist in a military department: I stay in government because I find my work interesting and challenging. I have had the opportunity to learn and travel and I still feel that there is a chance for advancement in my field.

Assistant regional director, cabinet department: I stay in government because I enjoy my work here and I feel I've better opportunity to use my skills, express myself here in the way in which I like to do it better than I would on the outside. I've had experience in both areas.

Why They Think People Leave

The entire group studied were asked: "What do you think are the main reasons that people in your field, at your level,[7] leave the federal service?"

[6] *Ibid.*, p. 512.
[7] The questionnaire for former employees used the words "in the top grades of the civil service" instead of "at your level."

The leading answers can be summed up in the words, "money," "new worlds to conquer," and "frustrations" (see Table 5.4).

"Money" is by far the most important reason given for "others" leaving the service.[8] The former employees, particularly the scientists and engineers, put significantly more emphasis on the "frustration" factor. This follows from the fact, reported in Table 5.2, that scientists and engineers give complexity and red tape as a primary cause of dissatisfaction. Another significant difference is the higher proportion of former employees who named "political reasons."

Why People Did Leave

Only the "new worlds to conquer" factor stood up when the questionnaires returned by former employees were analyzed. Their answers to the question "Why did you leave the federal service?" follow: [9]

	(N=80)
New opportunities, new kinds of work [10]	34%
Retirement (other reasons were undoubtedly contributing factors) [11]	32
Dissatisfaction with program, policies, colleagues, frustrations	20
"Political reasons"	14
More money	10
Forced out	7
Health reasons	5
Other	4

It is hard to label any individual reasons for leaving as "typical." The following are illustrative:

Research executive, Cabinet department: To accept offer involving total management responsibilities and direction of business, financial, and plant management of expanding liberal arts college.

[8] Remarks about money, both here and elsewhere in the interviews, were often accompanied by comments on the high cost of college education. This subject was also mentioned by some in connection with retirement plans: ". . . when my third son finishes college."

[9] Some respondents gave more than one reason.

[10] This was the reason most often given by respondents aged 45 to 49.

[11] This was the most frequent reason given by those aged 60 to 64 and 65 to 69.

TABLE 5.4 *Why Respondents Think Others Leave Higher Civil Service*

Reasons	PRESENT EMPLOYEES			FORMER EMPLOYEES		
	Scientific, Engineering, and Technical (N = 114)	Other (N = 149)	Total (N = 263)	Scientific, Engineering, and Technical (N = 30)	Other (N = 50)	Total (N = 80)
More money	69%	71%	70%	60%	54%	56%
New opportunities; new kinds of work	22	31	27	23	34	30
"Frustrations" (red tape, budget process, slow decisions, etc.)	14	14	14	57	34	43
"Few leave except to retire"	24	27	25	10	10	10
"Political reasons"	2	7	5	23	24	24

Medical officer, Cabinet department: To return to university setting—and private practice. Government too rigid and boring.

Top management expert, Cabinet department: The opportunity to build a professional clientele, and to acquire part ownership in the business, coupled with a substantial increase in remuneration.

Special assistant, Cabinet department: Forced out by Democratic administration.

The "more money" reason was most important in another very small but very important group surveyed. These were "outstanding top-level career people who left federal service" named in the "management" interviews. The author interviewed ten of these former officials—all of them occupying important positions in private industry or commerce. The desire to make more money was the only factor in five cases and the primary factor in two more. One left because of annoyance with internal organization politics, and the ninth resigned because he felt the need to face new challenges. The tenth left because of a change of administration.

WOULD THEY RETURN? In reply to the question "Under what circumstances would you return to federal service?" only 17 out of the 80 who answered said "under no circumstances." The rest gave a great variety of conditions, most of them emphasizing either more interesting or less frustrating work. Others wanted more pay or responsibility. Fifteen said they would return if needed in a national emergency. Thirteen would be willing to serve as consultants for brief periods.

These are typical of the replies of those who would return to a more interesting or higher position:

Engineer, Cabinet department: If pay scale is increased to somewhere near industry in top grades and if administrative procedures are cleared of a lot of unnecessary red tape and incompetent personnel.

Program executive, Cabinet department: Where broad and diversified . . . management experience, in and out of government, might be utilized in initiating new programs, strengthening and improving on-going programs, and providing leadership in programs identified with human welfare, security, and progress.

Would They Be Better Off Outside Government?

Employees were asked, "If you stayed in your present occupational field but left the federal government, do you think you would be better off or worse off than you are now? Why? (Consider pay, fringe benefits, rate of advancement, quality of leadership, opportunity to use skills, working conditions, professional atmosphere, and other factors.)"

Many stated that pay would be better outside the government [12] but that most other factors would *not* be better (see Table 5.5).

TABLE 5.5 *Views of Present Employees on Whether They Would Be Better Off or Worse Off Outside Government*

Category	Percentage (N = 246)
Better off outside:	
Generally better off	7%
Better money	50
Fringe benefits better	7
Other things better	9
Worse off outside:	
Generally worse off	39
Fringe benefits worse	17
Professional atmosphere worse	15
Other things worse	28
Not much difference; advantages balance	11

[12] This factor is also emphasized in the *Image* study. See Kilpatrick *et al.*, *Source Book*, p. 243.

Differences in responses between the scientific and engineering group and the "other" group were not significant.

These judgments can be checked against what former employees actually found when they took jobs outside the federal service (see Table 5.6).

TABLE 5.6 *Answers of Former Employees to "How Does Your Present Job Compare with Your Last Federal Job?"*

Category	Number Answering [a]	Better	Worse	About the Same
Pay	48	71%	12%	17%
Fringe benefits	43	44	28	28
Prospects of advancement	39	62	5	33
Opportunity to use skills	47	53	15	32
Quality of leadership	43	49	21	30

[a] The high proportion of nonresponses results from the fact that 23 of the 80 questioned were not employed, and 16 were self-employed.

The pay definitely proved to be better. In other respects, too, the nonfederal jobs were considered better than one would have expected from the views summarized in Table 5.5.

Replacements—Not Considered a Problem

A strong pattern of either contentment (or defensiveness?) emerged from employees' answers to "iffy" questions about replacements for themselves.

The first question was "If you should leave your present position for any reason, from what source would your replacement probably come?" The sources of replacement mentioned were:

	(N = 248)
From within the agency	71%
From another government agency	4
From outside the government	7
Not sure; don't know	14
Other replies	4

To the follow-up question "How satisfactory would you expect this replacement to be?" they replied:

	(N = 216)
Excellent, very good, quite satisfactory	76%
Fair, average	13
Poor	4
Can't say; no opinion	7

Asked "What changes, if any, are needed in the system for providing such replacements?," 35 percent (out of 158) said there was no problem, that no changes were needed. Other responses included:

	(N = 158)
Better training	17%
Mobility; rotation; "cross-fertilization"	8
Better recruiting	8
Higher salaries	8

The remaining comments were widely scattered.

Advice to the Young

In an effort to obtain a broad summary judgment on federal careers, the entire group studied were asked, "If a young person in your field came to you for advice as to whether he should follow a federal career leading to such a position as your own, how would you advise him? Why?"

The answers (see Table 5.7) tended to be affirmative, but those from the former employees were significantly more negative. Among present employees the scientists and engineers were definitely less favorable.

The "yes" answers varied from high endorsements to somewhat luke-warm suggestions that government offered security. Many were qualified by such comments as "if he had the right qualifications and education" or "if he were able, bright, public-service oriented, and not interested in making a lot of money" or "if he were willing to work hard, with little personal recognition or a large salary." A few insisted that he ought to have a "strong missionary bent."

TABLE 5.7. *Advisability of a Young Person's Following a Career Leading to "Such a Position as Your Own"*

Advice	PRESENT EMPLOYEES			FORMER EMPLOYEES		
	Scientific, Engineering, and Technical (N = 118)	Other (N = 145)	Total (N = 263)	Scientific, Engineering, and Technical (N = 27)	Other (N = 44)	Total (N = 71)
Yes (should follow such a career)	46%	60%	54%	30%	39%	35%
No (should not)	8	6	7	22	25	24
Depends on individual	28	16	21	11	18	15
Wouldn't advise; would point out good and bad features and let him decide	3	3	3	4	—	1
Get varied experience, both inside and outside government	2	3	3	7	5	6
Try outside first; then consider government	8	4	6	11	2	6
Own field limited, but try another part of government	—	4	2	—	2	1
Yes, but not necessarily for a full career	5	3	4	15	9	11

The category "Depends on the individual" also contained various qualifying statements. Instead of saying, "Yes, if he is qualified," some answers started, "If he wants to make a lot of money, no," and continued, "but if he wants an interesting life and won't be frustrated by slowness of achievement, yes." A very few had a different slant: "If he is capable and aggressive (ambitious, promising, exceptional), no. If he is the journeyman type (will only get midway or less, is easy-going, mediocre), yes."

The following comments are in sharp contrast—a strong endorsement and the dullest of thuds:

Project officer in a military department: I would ask any young man who might be interested in my advice first of all what his values are, and if it develops that he is top-notch and is highly motivated, I would say yes, he should join the government. But I would advise against joining the federal government service if he is simply looking for a job and more money.

Staff engineering expert in a military department: Positively "No." There is no spiritual reward, and only modest financial reward.

Dealing with Substandard Employees

The employee questionnaires raised a difficult question: "What should be done to deal effectively with employees in the top grades whose job performance does not measure up to expectations?"

Most of the 97 employees who answered the question suggested more than one solution, or rather a succession of solutions. Typically, they said one should try to talk to the employee about his difficulties, suggest training, or arrange for reassignment before attempting more drastic action. The majority seemed to believe that such instances occurred because of poor placement, and that most employees did not arrive at the top levels without having some high abilities which should be utilized, if not in their present job, then in other jobs.

One scientist said that nothing should be done; that probably such a person had produced effectively in his day ". . . and should be allowed to finish out his term in an administrative job." [13]

The actual count of comments resulted in this percentage distribution:

	(N = 97)
Reassign; shift to another job, downgrade	64%
Remove; force separation, transfer out	35
Counsel employee; re-evaluate his abilities	22
Urge or force early retirement	18
Provide further training	16
Very difficult; nothing can be done	5
Promote others around them	2

Changes Needed in Personnel Administration

Toward the end of each interview or questionnaire respondents were asked what changes they would make in personnel policies and methods affecting top federal jobs.[14]

[13] Such gratuitous insults were happily rare.

[14] Through a methodological fault, the wording of the question in the interviews was different from that in the questionnaires. Interviews: "If you had a free

Such a wide-open invitation produced comments that are difficult to quantify. They varied in intensity and in thoughtfulness as much as they did in subject matter. Nevertheless, some topics were mentioned much more often than others, and there was considerable agreement on the need for certain improvements. No single suggestion was mentioned by a majority of the total group studied. Although the question implied that changes should be suggested, 9 percent of the employees said that no changes were needed.

Recruitment, Selection, Promotion, Transfer

The largest number of suggestions were about the processes of filling jobs. The main themes stressed were recognition of genuine merit for jobs to be filled, speed and flexibility, and decentralization of authority.

Some 15 percent of the total group urged some form of rank-in-person plan, many mentioning either the Senior Civil Service plan of the Second Hoover Commission [15] or the "earned status" plan proposed by Rufus E. Miles, Jr.,[16] a plan which would protect the grades and salaries of employees assigned to lower-grade work for a variety of reasons. The reason most frequently given was the desirability of making reassignments without encountering the inflexibilities of position classification. These suggestions were made much more by the "other" group than by the scientists and engineers.

A slightly larger percentage recommended more effective systems to encourage mobility—both within and between agencies—in order to develop staff and to meet program needs.

A high defense planning executive: . . . ———is really quite strong on the need and desirability of a career officer system. He thinks that a system in which it was expected and normal and

---

hand to change personnel policies or methods for the top grades of the federal civil service, what are some of the main things you would do?" Questionnaires: "If you had a free hand to plan a personnel system for the top grades of the federal civil service, what are some of the main features you would put in it?"

[15] Commission on Organization of the Executive Branch of the Government: (1) *Personnel and Civil Service* (Government Printing Office, 1955), pp. 37–44; and (2) Task Force on Personnel and Civil Service, *Report on Personnel and Civil Service* (Government Printing Office, 1955), pp. 49–62.

[16] Rufus E. Miles, Jr., "An 'Earned Status' Proposal," reprinted from *Civil Service Journal*, April–June 1961.

probably required that people would spend say three to five years on an assignment and then be moved out would make things really easier for everybody. The executives themselves would be shaken loose to get the kinds of experience they need, it would be easier to sandwich in educational and training assignments, and the expectation of movement would make movement more convenient both for the executives and for the agencies.

With regard to recruitment it was frequently urged that recruiters be authorized to make speedy job commitments to outstanding prospects.

Improvements in promotion systems were urged by about 20 percent, particularly by scientists and engineers among the former employees. Those who made such comments generally did not make specific proposals but tended to ask that something be done about eliminating seniority, number of employees supervised,[17] arbitrary time factors, and "personal factors" as considerations in promotions. A few strongly recommended that promotion review boards be established. Examples of comments:

> An agricultural specialist: More opportunity for career advancement without jeopardizing the career status by having to go into Schedule C positions. Opportunity for advancement or increased salary scale to retain outstanding personnel. Some kind of regular review or consideration should be given for advancement of professional people other than routine advancement as at present.

> Attorney in a Cabinet department: More attention should be given to professional services of individuals rather than the number of people supervised as a basis for promotion. The need for some way to give chiefs in the specialized area a free hand is important.

Classification and Pay

About half the total group expressed themselves on classification and pay. The most popular theme (emphasized by 33 percent of present employees and 20 percent of former employees) was greater flexibility in adjusting salaries at "supergrade" levels. Some suggested abandonment of position classification at such levels and substitution

---

[17] This factor was mentioned in connection with upward reclassifications.

of "the Public Law 313 approach." [18] Others recommended abolition of quota limitations on "supergrade" positions:

Head of a very large program division in a Cabinet department: We should remove the arbitrary limitations on the upper grades. We should try to get the pay structure and the benefits which are comparable with industry. . . . We should be able to bring in people at the career level who would not have to make financial sacrifices, particularly in the field of research, medicine, and such people as a professor from a university. We have had to resort at times to contractual arrangements in order to get work done and in order to get around the limitations and to have flexibility.

Higher salary levels (sometimes phrased as "adequate salaries" or "salaries competitive with industry") were called for by about 20 percent.[19] A significant number said that there should be larger salary differentials between higher and lower grades in the civil service.

Engineering executive, independent agency: Bit by bit we have reached a point where several grades are bunched together, and many individuals have come up under this lid and are stuck there. We have a vast number earning practically the same salaries, with differences of only about five hundred dollars between the level of Assistant Director and Director, and that is wrong. If we can find some way to lift that, a larger spread of salaries in the top levels would seem to me very sensible and reasonable.

A few called for more generous provisions for relocation expenses, travel, and official entertainment.

Training

Training proposals, made by over 20 percent of the group, can be summarized as "Do more." They were about equally divided among these categories:

Provide for sabbatical leaves or special training assignments
Provide continuing training programs at top levels
Use career planning and development programs
Various other proposals, including a "civil service academy"

[18] Salary setting without grading for scientific and engineering positions.
[19] These comments were made before the substantial salary increases of 1964 were enacted.

Dismissals

On this subject as on most of the others, the former employees were more vocal than present employees. Twenty-one percent of the former employees and 8 percent of the present employees commented. For the most part they wanted simpler dismissal procedures, but a few proposed use of a "selection out" system.

"Politics"

One out of every four of the former employees (but 9 percent of the present employees) wanted less "politics." The most common statement was that politics should be eliminated as a consideration in selection at these levels. About half of those who commented on "politics" believe that "supergrades" should be reserved for career employees and that Schedule C [20] should be eliminated. Such comments seemed to brush aside the need for having top jobs which can be filled by new persons in whom incoming political executives have confidence. The other half expressed resentment of political partisanship in personnel decisions—a much more defensible view.

Other Ideas

Scores of other proposals were made, most of them thoughtful, but none by a significant number of individuals. Some of the topics included:

Liberalized retirement
More valid performance rating system
Special personnel systems for scientific and professional employees

Some of the "suggestions" turned out to be generalized comments about the attitude of Congress or the image of the federal service.

[20] Positions of a confidential or policy determining character, whose incumbents may be expected to change in the event of a political transition.

"Anything Else You Would Like To Say?"

The interviewees and those who filled out the questionnaires were given a chance to add any other comments. Some said nothing; some reiterated statements on the topics about which they felt most strongly; and some made comments (usually appreciative or interested) about the present study. Others pronounced some interesting benedictions:

I hope this all serves some useful purpose.
I served 37 years and loved every one of them.
Lousy! Too much politics!
Don't forget how much the federal government has improved in 25–50 years.
I am as happy as a pig in the poke.

Summary

The higher civil servants covered by this chapter are dedicated to their work and to the public service, and generally well satisfied. They would be inclined to advise young people to follow careers like their own. Their main dissatisfactions center on governmental bigness, caution, and red tape. They have a high opinion of the effectiveness of their agencies and of the competence of their colleagues.

They think people leave the higher civil service for more money. Many of those who actually left did so for new challenges, and would return to federal service under favorable circumstances. Those still in the service believe that they could be replaced by able people from within their agencies.

Finally, they suggest improvements in the personnel system, particularly with respect to the filling of jobs and the setting of salaries.

6

What Can Be Done?
Analysis of the Findings

THE FACTS and judgments presented in the previous three chapters have not clearly pointed to remedies or reforms. The data show a stable, well-qualified group of civil servants, well regarded by their superiors and generally well-satisfied themselves.[1] Both they and their bosses have ideas about changes that should be made, but it is difficult to find agreement on possible lines of action.

There is no real basis, however, for either complacent or frustrated inaction. The quality of the higher civil service is so vitally important to the nation that efforts to raise its personnel system to a higher level of excellence are strongly needed. These efforts obviously must be exerted long before the employees concerned reach the top grades. A higher civil service of top quality is not likely unless there is top quality in the middle and lower grades.

The need for action also becomes clearer when the findings are evaluated against criteria for an effective personnel system.[2] This chapter offers such an evaluation. It discusses each element of the personnel system, pointing up the merits and disadvantages of possible courses of action. Most of these possibilities are not new, but it will be helpful to take a fresh look at them in the light of this study.

[1] To add a subjective note: The project interviewers returned from nearly all of their interviews enthusiastic about the apparent competence and dedication of members of the higher federal civil service.

[2] See Chapter 2.

The Needs of the Future

It is a rare personnel study that does not recommend a system (or an improved system) for forecasting manpower needs and for planning to meet them.[3] Such planning is something that always has to be done, or done better, in any personnel system. The present report is not abnormal in this respect.

Summary of Findings

Some agencies have reported success in working toward effective forecasting and inventory systems (see Chapter 4). Other agencies are frankly dissatisfied, and there is as yet no governmentwide plan for forecasting personnel needs. This deficiency was emphatically noted in the *Image* study.[4]

Definite progress on this forecasting problem is now being made by the Bureau of Programs and Standards of the Civil Service Commission, which is preparing to issue its first tentative projections of future manpower needs arranged by occupational groups. The Commission figures cover about one million positions in 160 occupational groups. They will show personnel gains and losses for each group over a one-year period. For entry-level jobs the "gains" data will show what percent the government received of graduating classes in a particular occupation (e.g., mechanical engineering). Figures on anticipated gains and losses will be projected for the budget year (i.e., the fiscal year following the current one) and the three following budget years.

This project will provide a useful basis for overall recruitment planning by the Commission and the agencies. The data will not be pre-

[3] See, for example, Recommendation 12 of the Herter Report, *Personnel for the New Diplomacy: Report of the Committee on Foreign Affairs Personnel* (Carnegie Endowment for International Peace, December 1962, p. 63); Recommendation 1 in the "Personnel Operations" section of the Folsom Report, *Report of the Advisory Committee on Public Health Service Personnel Systems* (U.S. Department of Health, Education, and Welfare, March 1962, p. 7); and David T. Stanley and associates, *Professional Personnel for the City of New York* (Brookings Institution, 1963, p. 6).

[4] Franklin P. Kilpatrick, Milton C. Cummings, Jr., and M. Kent Jennings, *The Image of the Federal Service* (Brookings Institution, 1964), pp. 249–50.

sented in enough detail, however, to show occupational needs by grade levels or by agencies.

It will be up to the individual agencies to plan for their higher civil service needs by assembling data on retirement eligibility and other anticipated turnover in the upper grades, and by forecasting the personnel resources that will meet these needs. Widespread progress will take considerable effort, especially since some agency officials, as reported in Chapter 4, are satisfied with their planning in this respect.

It was not feasible for the present study to make agency-by-agency evaluations. Some agencies may have this matter well in hand. From the standpoint of the service as a whole, however, there is basis for grave concern. The basis for concern lies in these facts: (1) About half of the higher civil service can retire in 5 to 10 years, and mean to. (2) An additional number of employees in grades 15 through 18 can be expected to resign or die within 10 years. (3) Planning and inventory methods are in an early stage of development.

Possible Courses of Action

There is no defensible alternative to more vigorous development of a governmentwide forecasting and inventory program for the higher civil service. At present agency programs are spotty, and the Civil Service Commission inventory is just getting started. All agencies should be *directed* by the President to make five-year forecasts of future needs; to relate these to anticipated turnover; and to demonstrate that they have tangible recruitment and development activities operating on a scale that will meet the needs. The Civil Service Commission can issue standards covering forecasting and inventory programs, prepare prototype programs, and as part of its inspection work, check the adequacy of agency programs.

Competition for Professionals and Executives

Summary of Findings

IN GENERAL. How well has the government met the competition of other employers? How well has it staffed the top grades with superior personnel? These are difficult questions. They call for judgments of quality that can be made only profession by profession, program by program. Even so, it is hard to establish standards for such judgments.

The present study, which did not establish such standards and did not seek outside-the-government judgments, can give only a partial and mixed answer. Government officials, whether responding as "management" or as "employees," do not perceive "serious difficulty." More than 40 percent of the management interviewees denied there was a problem. Many of the others spoke of recruitment difficulties in shortage fields, or of inequitable salary levels, or of the loss of outstanding employees, some at top levels, some "on their way up." Yet there was no clear prevailing tone of deep concern. This attitude, this lack of a basis for driving effort to secure only the best, is a problem in itself.

Unofficial preliminary statistics in the GS-15 to 18 levels also do not clearly demonstrate "serious difficulty" in retaining personnel.

These appraisals of the present situation assume that the government will continue its present policies of contracting out billions of dollars worth of research and development work. These policies are based in part on the belief that the government could *not* have the skills needed on an "in house" basis.

SOME PROBLEMS. Interviews and group discussions identified the following problems as needing attention:

1. There is little central direction of recruitment policy or effort, either from the Executive Office or from the Civil Service Commission.

2. Formal recruitment efforts are largely directed at junior levels. Higher level recruitment is done largely by program executives. In the field of administration the Federal Administrative Management Examination (FAME) at grades GS-12 through 14 is an expensive [5] and uncritical method of qualifying applicants chosen by the agencies.

3. Federal recruiters, unlike many recruiters in private industry, are unable to make on-the-spot or rapid commitments to prospects because of examining and appointment procedures.

Possible Courses of Action

PRESENT SITUATION. One can defend present patterns and methods of federal recruitment by maintaining, "We're doing pretty well. Don't

[5] One official in a position to know estimated that FAME costs the Commission $100,000 a year.

rock the boat." The present system has staffed the higher civil service in a way that is fairly satisfactory to its members and their bosses. As recruitment problems arise they must be met by those responsible for program results—a logical arrangement.

Yet reliance on present patterns and methods has disadvantages and dangers. For one thing, as already noted, there is little evidence of a driving overall concern for total improvement, led from a central source. Second, federal employment lacks appeal to executives and professionals in contrast with nonfederal employment.[6] Third, there are inflexibilities in present methods that could be remedied (e.g., delays in rating tests and announcing results, and requirements of higher-echelon approval of appointment actions). Fourth, there are assumptions, not completely valid, that most recruitment should be directed at lower levels and that most higher positions should be filled from within the agency. Fifth, most recruitment is motivated by the needs of particular agency programs; it is not based on a concern to build a higher civil service of greatest value to the government as a whole. On this last point, one can argue that the entire government is well staffed if the various agencies are well staffed. Nevertheless, short-term considerations will tend to control such a fragmented approach and will work against the selection of persons of broad capacities and usefulness.

CENTRAL LEADERSHIP FOR RECRUITMENT. These disadvantages prevail despite strong efforts by the Civil Service Commission to attract high-quality college graduates and to assist the agencies with recruiting problems. Stronger recruitment for the higher civil service, as well as for positions which lead to it, could be aided by establishment of a special central organization for this purpose within the Civil Service Commission. An alternative possibility is the assignment of this work to a special organization in the White House or the Executive Office of the President.[7] It would be tangible evidence of the President's desire to attract superior professionals and executives to federal service.

No matter where it is placed, the establishment of a point of central

[6] Kilpatrick *et al.*, *op. cit.*, p. 247 and elsewhere.

[7] See Chapter 7 for a broader discussion of how federal personnel administration can be organized.

leadership for professional and executive recruitment would have several advantages. First, it could coordinate recruitment efforts for agencies seeking the same types of scarce personnel. Second, such an office could bring pressures on agencies to improve the quality of their recruitment programs and to reduce delays in appointment procedures. Third, it could help obtain more effective public support for federal recruitment—possibly through the medium of a distinguished advisory committee.

Such an office would have to avoid burdening agencies with less-than-productive reports and meetings, or attempting an unrealistic degree of coordination. Its success would be measured by its ability to devise new approaches to problem areas, raise the general level of recruitment effort, and improve the government's competitive position.

NEW DIRECTIONS IN RECRUITMENT EFFORT. The present study yielded suggestions for the following recruitment approaches that could be added to present programs or made part of the work of a new central recruitment office:

1. An energetic effort to recruit superior people with 3 to 10 years' nonfederal experience at GS–11 to 15 levels. They may be found in private industry, academic institutions, nonprofit organizations, and state or municipal governments. This effort would bring into the federal government people of top quality, with new perspective, and add to the supply of excellent "back-up" material for the higher civil service. The program should seek people who may prefer the breadth and challenge of federal service to whatever they have found in their present work. It must find them before they feel "locked in" by fringe benefits and development programs.

2. An equally energetic effort to recruit short-term higher civil service employees to meet particular urgent needs. Such recruitment is common for Schedule C and sub-Cabinet posts but not for the "career" service. Short-term service is now encouraged by civil service regulations [8] but is little used. Such recruitment could be beneficial as part of an interchange plan with selected nongovernmental organizations that work closely with the federal government.

[8] Sec. 2.303 now permits "term" appointments for positions of limited duration, not to exceed four years.

Evaluating Performance and Potential

Summary of Findings

Systematic evaluation or ranking of candidates is required both for appointment and for promotion. Employees are evaluated for awards and, in many cases, for assignment to desirable training opportunities.

A strong flavor of personal, subjective evaluations was apparent in the interviews and questionnaires of this study. This is inevitable. People's evaluation of people *is* personal and subjective. What is questionable is the absence of a more solid, dependable basis for the development and selection of higher civil servants.

Possible Courses of Action

PRESENT SITUATION. Present evaluation requirements, as set forth in the *Federal Personnel Manual,* are not likely to accomplish the desired results. Agencies are required to establish performance rating plans for purposes which may include, among others, guidance for promotions and identifying training needs.[9] Such plans normally achieve little because of the requirement that they result in a summary adjective rating of Outstanding, Satisfactory, or Unsatisfactory. With respect to merit promotion plans it is required that qualification standards and evaluation methods shall be—

Reasonable
Applied with fairness and equity to all candidates
Developed with the intent of obtaining the highest practicable degree of validity and reliability under the specific circumstances.[10]

And ". . . there should be adequate emphasis on those qualifications which indicate a candidate's potential for future promotion."[11]

It seems clear that something more compelling is needed to help select and develop superior executives and professionals for higher civil service jobs.

[9] *Federal Personnel Manual,* Chap. 430, p. 5.
[10] *Ibid.,* Chap. 335, p. 9.
[11] *Ibid.,* Chap. 335, p. 11.

MORE EXACTING REQUIREMENTS. A minimum approach would be to require all agencies to prepare and use evaluation methods for their development and promotion programs (not merely for the higher civil service but also for positions leading to it) which contain at least the following features:

1. Judgments on the level to which the employee is expected to develop and on the type of assignments for which he is best suited.

2. Specific recommendations, in appropriate cases, for the employee to be reassigned, placed in a specific type of training program, given an award, or for other action.

3. Inclusion of detailed comment with evidence or examples, where possible, of the employee's ability to take responsibility; adaptability to new assignments; ability to complete assignments within deadlines; initiative; innovative capacity; skill in supervision; analytical and critical capacity; ability to synthesize; ability to write incisively; ability to negotiate; and so on.

4. Development and pretesting of evaluation devices by persons professionally qualified for this type of work.

5. Evaluation by at least three informed persons.

6. Use of evaluations in considering employees for training assignments, promotions, incentive awards, and other actions.

7. Preparation of new evaluations when there is a change in supervision or a significant change in duties.

Particular emphasis should be laid on the research aspects of this effort. Agencies should be strongly encouraged to use the best minds in the personnel psychology field to develop and try out more valid and predictive evaluation systems. Interagency consultations on progress and problems should prove valuable.

If evaluations are to be effective, the content will have to be confidential and withheld from the employee concerned. Otherwise those who do the evaluating will tend to make bland or overgenerous statements. Frank statements which do not conform to the employee's idea of himself will cause defensiveness and strained relations. The employee can and should be talked to about the *results* of evaluations: plans for transfers, training he should take, and other steps that affect him, but he need not see the evaluation itself.

EVALUATION BY PERSONS OUTSIDE THE EMPLOYING AGENCY. A more ambitious alternative might call for evaluations (having the same features as those in the foregoing list) to be made with the aid of a panel consisting of two or three agency representatives, a Civil Service Commission representative, and a nongovernment person (perhaps a distinguished former government official). These evaluations could be made on all persons in, and proposed for, the top four grades and could be filed for use by the Civil Service Commission. Formal consideration of such evaluations could be made compulsory for all transfers and promotions in the higher civil service.

Such a plan would have the advantage of adding objectivity and formality to the process and of having more data available on higher civil servants being considered for other assignments. Its disadvantages are (1) an increase in time and expense required; and (2) the questionable value of judgments made by persons who do not have a working relationship with the employee or a direct responsibility for his supervision.

Training and Development

This area of the problem is baffling because of the unanswerable question, "How much is enough?" People are never trained to their maximum potential. There never seem to be enough resources to meet even the more common training needs. One can apply a rule of reason.

Summary of Findings

FORMAL TRAINING PROGRAMS. In this study there was no intensive effort to probe management's experience with training. Interview comments were inconclusive but pointed to considerable activity in short courses and seminars. A little under half of the employees interviewed had taken formal training at government expense and commented on it favorably.

The government's formal training activities for civilian employees (both in-service and outside the government) are impressive in scope, variety, resources used, and number of employees taking part. The Civil Service Commission's 1963 annual report shows that $35 million were spent during the fiscal year on training activities—or about $14 per employee on the federal payroll.

The Commission's Office of Career Development was established in 1960 to stimulate training and development activities. Among its many other activities the Office sponsors a variety of short courses suited to the needs of all agencies, such as courses in general management or in automatic data processing. During fiscal year 1964 the Commission conducted 37 courses for 1,188 career executives in grades GS–14 through 18.[12]

The departments and agencies also offer a variety of technical and management courses, many of which are open to employees of other agencies. Such courses, along with those sponsored by the Commission, are listed in a catalog issued by the Office of Career Development. The latest issue includes more than two hundred courses. A few samples indicate the variety available:

Food Microbiology
Radioactive Pollutants in the Environment
Management Institute for Supervisory Scientists and Engineers
Top Management Seminar
Communist Strategy: Its Basis in Theory and Practice
Public Problems and Federal Programs

The Civil Service Commission also established an Executive Seminar Center at Kings Point, New York, to provide off-the-job development conferences for employees in GS grades 14 and 15. The trainees usually attend for two-week periods. A recent report by the Chairman of the Commission on the Center's first year of operation cited highly favorable comments both by trainees and by visiting faculty. More intensive evaluation studies have been started.

Thus there are short courses available to fill many gaps in employees' skills and knowledge and to provide needed background.

There is a lack, however, of long-term off-the-job training and development. There are few civilian employee equivalents of the military practice of assigning an officer to a year or two of postgraduate study at a leading university, or to nine months at the National War College.[13]

<hr />

[12] *Actions To Improve the Higher Civil Service* (unpublished outline), U.S. Civil Service Commission, July 2, 1964.

[13] Currently 31 civilian employees each year attend the National War College,

During fiscal year 1963 only minuscule percentages of employees
were assigned to long-term (more than 120 days) training: [14]

GRADE	NUMBER OF EMPLOYEES
GS-16	2
GS-15	22
GS-14	40
GS-13	64
GS-12	59
GS-11	66
GS-10	2
GS- 9	64
GS- 8	5
GS- 7	40
GS- 6	1
GS- 5	2
Total	367

By contrast the typical colonel or Navy captain or one-star officer
will have spent prolonged periods in advanced schooling. Some management interviewees in the Department of Defense noted that as a
result officers tend to show judgment of greater maturity and breadth
than do civilians at comparable levels. (This could result from varied
and responsible career assignments as well as from formal education.)

The present level of long-term training for higher federal civil
servants looks like a drop in the bucket. Its inadequacy is strongly
suggested by the personnel needs for the dynamic and technical nature
of federal programs—and by comparison with the military officer
program.

A number of interviewees said that federal executives simply cannot
spare the manpower or money to meet these long-term training needs.
One high official (in a well-financed large department) said, "If I show
I can spare a man for a year the budget boys will want to abolish his
job." By contrast, military manning tables are so planned as to allow
for training assignments.

THE "BACK-UP" SITUATION. A large majority of the employees interviewed said that they could be satisfactorily replaced from within their

---

and 33 attend the Industrial College of the Armed Forces. The number of "spaces"
available for civilian employees has been increased gradually in recent years.

[14] U.S. Civil Service Commission, Office of Career Development, *Long-Term
Training in Non-Government Facilities, Fiscal Year 1963*, p. 4.

agencies—a comment that suggests a satisfactory development situation. The "management" group were less sanguine but still favorable. More than half of them said that their higher civil service people were well "backed up." Note, however, that 35 percent said that they were "backed up" poorly, or not as well as they should be. This last judgment, considered with the intention-to-retire data in Chapter 3, raises serious doubts about the "bench strength" of the higher civil service team.

NARROW DEVELOPMENT PATTERNS. Chapter 3 also demonstrated the occupational and organizational narrowness of the higher civil servants' experience. (More than 85 percent had worked in one or two agencies; there was little interchange between headquarters and field; and few had left and returned to federal service.) Mobility as a means of development can be overdone, but the narrowness of the experience shown is undesirable. Every job in a different organization gives the employee a new body of knowledge, affects his skills, and adds a new perspective. All these qualifications he takes with him to future jobs, which are benefited by the understanding he has gained. Increased mobility is basic to the development of the truly superior executive or professional in federal service.

Interagency mobility is more questionable in the case of a bench scientist working on a long-term series of experiments or an administrator of a very specialized program activity. Even in these cases, however, it is difficult to question the value of the perspective that would be gained from a temporary assignment to another organization for training purposes.

Possible Courses of Action

CONTINUING PRESENT TRENDS. The present direction of effort in the development of higher civil servants is difficult to criticize. Training and development programs have been accepted as necessary elements of management, and there is steady growth in the number, variety, and apparent quality of such programs. Some new lines of progress could be begun, however, in the never-ending effort to develop superior professionals and executives. These are not substitutes for present programs.

MORE LONG-TERM TRAINING ASSIGNMENTS. The present reluctance to assign employees to outside institutions for full semesters or full academic years results from timidity, budget limitations, and work pressures. All might be overcome by insistent executive leadership. Agency heads could be required by the President to assign no fewer than a stated percentage of employees at stated levels to universities or other institutions for training of value to the agency program. The percentage would be low, and the employees would be selected competitively by a representative high-level board. Salaries would be continued and all necessary educational and moving expenses paid by the government. Every effort would be made to promote employees upon their return—or to assign them to positions they consider desirable, if promotion vacancies were not immediately available. (Alternatively, promotion to "supergrade" level could be made contingent upon satisfactory completion of a required course.)

Such training assignments would be provided for in advance in preparing budgets and manning tables.[15] To finance these training assignments agencies could either be encouraged to increase their budgets within prescribed limits or be compelled to absorb costs.

INTERAGENCY DEVELOPMENTAL ASSIGNMENTS. To meet the need for broader career development and varied perspectives, agency heads could be required by the President to work out interagency assignments for a few of their most promising executives and professionals. (Here again stronger central leadership is required.) Such assignments are most likely to be successful when—

1. They are obviously relevant to the employee's career and to the agency's needs.

2. Assignments are made on an interchange basis between agencies working in kindred fields, such as conservation and resource management, water research, recreation, enforcement of health standards, or oceanography.

[15] The Department of Defense has recently taken a step in this direction. A memorandum from the Deputy Secretary of Defense "to heads of the military departments and defense agencies requires the establishment of special pools of funds and manpower spaces earmarked for use in meeting long-term educational and training needs in the Department of Defense through periods of training in excess of 120 days for selected civilian officials and specialists. The plan will enable organizations to fill a trainee's position during his absence and guarantee the trainee, as a minimum, entitlement to return to his position after training." *Civil Service Journal*, Vol. 5 (July–September 1964), inside back cover.

3. They are made at a stage when employees' careers are more flexible than they would be later—say at GS-7 through 14—and last at least one year.

4. Employees are given promotion opportunities or desirable assignments upon their return.

5. All expenses are paid so that the employees are at no financial disadvantage.

In some cases difficulties might stem from qualification requirements or classification problems. The former can be overcome by training agreements approved in advance by the Civil Service Commission. Classification would seem a problem if an employee were assigned temporarily to a less responsible position. Civil service regulations, however, permit his salary to continue at the same level for up to two years if he is assigned to a lower grade "without prejudice."

The advantages of such increased mobility are broader perspective and increased knowledge from varied experience.[16] The disadvantages would be some loss in intensive intra-agency development and the administrative inconvenience and "wheel-spinning" resulting from the changes of personnel. A temporary drop in both individual and organization performance can be expected from personnel shifts, but this is simply part of the price to be paid for developing people.

The field of administration would be a fertile one for planned development through personnel rotation. A small group (perhaps 30) of employees in grades 9 to 12 with superior managerial potential could be chosen competitively and assigned to a centrally monitored development program to give them experience in several different agencies and on Capitol Hill. They would deliberately be given difficult tasks in order to "stretch" their abilities. Participating agencies would receive an employee in return for every one they gave up as the program proceeded. These trainees would be watched, evaluated, and counseled. They would be placed in GS-12 or 13 "target jobs" on completion of their training. If successful, this program could be expanded to cover more employees and higher grades.

OUTSIDE EXPERIENCE. Developmental mobility could also be extended to experience in state or local governments, nonprofit research organizations, educational institutions, or commercial or industrial organizations. Such assignments could provide invaluable training. A necessary

[16] See also the discussion of this point in Kilpatrick et al., op. cit., pp. 259-60.

prerequisite would be regulations and, if necessary, legislation to protect the tenure, pay, seniority, and benefits of employees so assigned. The assignments could be reserved for a limited number of employees at certain levels. They could be used partly like sabbatical leaves for senior personnel and partly for giving younger employees essential experience.

This type of training, like interagency assignments, will be resisted by supervisors who fear that the employees will never come back from the assignments. Such resistance can be overcome by providing for acceptable replacements and by constant education of supervisory officials.

A STAFF COLLEGE. The need for a federal educational institution for the higher civil service has been discussed for some years.[17] A plan put forward by the Civil Service Commission suggests that a federal staff college be established primarily for "supergrade" employees. The four-months' curriculum would emphasize broad problems of public policy, fundamentals of the democratic process, evaluation of administrative concepts, and interrelationships of government, business, education, and other institutions. The proposal contemplates a high-grade core faculty, visiting speakers, and an away-from-work location. Three alternative organization arrangements are suggested. Each contemplates support by private funds, augmented by federal tuition payments.[18]

Such an institution would be definitely beneficial in maintaining a superior higher civil service—primarily because of its ability to broaden the knowledge and understanding of a group whose experience is narrow. (Federal executives and professionals have already testified to the value of much briefer discussions of major public problems in the Advanced Study Program of the Brookings Institution.)

It would be possible to provide similar instruction and discussion in private educational institutions, but the federal staff college would have the following advantages:

1. Its program would be devised entirely for the benefit of federal employees, without being diverted by the educational needs of other students.

---

[17] See, for example, Society for Personnel Administration, *A Proposal for a Federal Administrative Staff College* (Washington, 1953), Pamphlet No. 5.
[18] "Plan for a Senior Staff College" in *University Federal Agency Conference on Career Development* (U.S. Civil Service Commission, 1961), pp. 19–A to 26.

2. The timing and content of—and resources for—its programs could be flexibly adjusted according to the program needs.

3. The institution could save money by using federal property.

Two main drawbacks can be foreseen:

1. A federal institution might have more difficulty than a private organization in maintaining a superior curriculum because of limitations in its policies or resources.

2. Extra expense and organizational effort would be required to start the college and keep it operating.

The present study cannot determine whether the advantages of a federal staff college over use of nongovernment institutions are great enough to justify the organizational effort and overhead expenses. Experience with the new Kings Point Executive Seminar Center should furnish some clues. The educational need for the program is clear, and the most suitable means can easily be determined, once the leadership of the executive branch decides to go ahead.

REQUIRED AGENCY PLANS. Another desirable step forward from the present situation would be a requirement that each agency prepare a plan for developing employees for the higher civil service primarily through planned work assignments. Plans would have to be approved by the Civil Service Commission and progress reviewed by that agency. Agency plans could include such elements as—

A major change (e.g., assignment to a materially different kind of work, to an extended period of outside training, or to field or overseas duty) at least three times in an employee's career.

Some lesser change (e.g., into a different organizational unit, to somewhat different duties, or even to a new location) often enough to provide stimulation and fresh experience and to avoid "going stale."

Interchange of employees between the regular civil service, excepted services, and special corps services.

Assignment to university education (long-term or short-term, according to the need) or to a federal staff college.

EASING GEOGRAPHICAL CHANGES. Moves from one geographical location to another—whether for development or other purposes—are handicapped by the financial burdens imposed on the employee. The government pays for his transportation and other travel expenses, for the transportation of his dependents, and, within limits, for moving his household effects. It does not pay for a variety of other expenses he may incur, such as a loss in selling his house, a mortgage penalty payment, lease-breaking costs, the price of new draperies, or temporary hotel rent until he finds a new home. These have become serious impediments to mobility. Many industrial organizations reimburse their employees for such expenses.

A partial remedy is offered by pending legislation introduced at the request of the Civil Service Commission. The bill would allow the government to raise the weight allowance on shipping household goods; pay up to three years' storage of such goods if the employee moves to a location where there are no residence quarters; and pay his family's expenses while traveling and while occupying temporary quarters up to 30 days. These changes will be helpful, but other types of relocation expenses will also have to be paid if employees are to be protected from losses.

DEVELOPMENT IN A JOB SYSTEM AND IN A CORPS SYSTEM. Under present circumstances it will always be difficult to arrange for substantial periods of outside training or for interagency or extragovernmental developmental assignments. Agency heads and their personnel officers are interested mainly in keeping jobs filled with qualified people. They have little incentive to send a higher civil servant away for training, particularly if he may never return. The employee himself may be reluctant to absent himself from his job and his agency, fearing loss of momentum or advantage in his career. In short, neither the agency head, the supervisor, the personnel officer, nor the employee himself is primarily motivated to build and maintain a high-quality civil service for the whole government.

A corps system by contrast offers increased incentives for personnel development, both to the employee and to management. The officer thinks of himself primarily as a member of the corps rather than as an incumbent of a job. His rank and pay depend more on his development and competence than on the billet he occupies. The agency head knows that an officer sent to a developmental assignment will be replaced by one of comparable status and competence. He knows also that such an assignment does not cause him budget and personnel ceiling problems. Under a corps system, then, both management and the officer have more of a stake in off-the-job training. Under the present civil service system, management's inclinations to keep the employee on the job must be overpowered if such training is to take place.[19]

Selection

Summary of Findings

As far as can be judged, federal executives have not done a bad selection job, but it has been a narrow and highly personal job—at least as far as the present higher civil service is concerned. GS–15 and "supergrade" jobs are filled mainly by promotion. Only 11 percent of the group studied here entered the service at or above GS–15. Selections reflect personal observation and acquaintanceship. The civil service "merit promotion" plans [20] have caused more candidates to be considered, and more systematically considered, but they have reinforced a tendency to fill jobs from within agencies.

Evaluation and ranking procedures are required to be systematic and objective, but specific methods are not prescribed by the Commission. Several of the agencies (as noted in Chapter 4) make periodic evaluations of employees who may be considered for higher-grade positions. In the agencies with more highly organized executive development programs, such evaluations are group judgments.

Consideration of candidates from other agencies or from outside the government is "urged" but not required. Agencies are encouraged to use the Career Executive Roster in filling "supergrade" jobs. From March 1961 to March 1963, 29 agencies asked for referrals in efforts to fill 134 positions.[21] Only a handful of placements were made. The operation of the Roster is handicapped by the facts that (1) no evaluative material is available and (2) the staff who operate it are unable to become acquainted with many members of the Roster and hence

[19] General advantages and disadvantages of corps systems are summarized in Chapter 7.

[20] Required by Chapter 335 of the *Federal Personnel Manual*.

[21] Mel H. Bolster, *Federal Career Executives: Three Years' Experience with the Career Executive Roster* (unpublished manuscript, April 1964), p. 13.

to do a real placement job. Thus the Commission's assistance cannot be considered a strong factor in filling higher civil service jobs.[22]

Possible Courses of Action

PRESENT SITUATION. The present pattern of filling higher civil service jobs is well accepted on the whole by management and employees. One must acknowledge that it has selected people of competence and dedication. Efforts to change it would be regarded as disruptive, burdensome, or threatening. Nevertheless, the present pattern has had a tendency to fill jobs with persons of narrow rather than broad experience; and it has encouraged selection of a nearby, available employee rather than searching for a truly superior candidate.[23]

The present situation also puts an unreasonable burden on any civil servant (higher *or* lower) who feels that he needs to make a change. He must scout around from agency to agency to find out what jobs are available and what their requirements are; he leaves a Form 57 at each agency where he feels encouraged, and follows up from time to time to see what his chances are. This "process" is patently wasteful and unsystematic.

CENTRALLY CONTROLLED SELECTIONS. One alternative would be to withdraw appointment authority from agency heads for specified higher positions (perhaps all "supergrades") and establish a central staff or board to control selections for these positions. Such a plan would be analogous to plans used in selecting higher officers in the military services and other career corps systems.

A central system, supported by good staff work, records, and evaluation procedures, offers some advantages over the present pattern. It would reduce such subjective factors as proximity and friendship and increase objectivity in screening and selection. It would reduce the danger of overlooking an excellent candidate in another agency. It would offer a means of ready reassignment of an employee who was poorly placed or utilized in his present job. Perhaps most important of

[22] At this writing Commission staff members are developing a new system for selecting, reassigning, and releasing "supergrade" executives.

[23] According to some interviewees, this results in a selection criterion called, "We really can't pass over old Joe, can we?"

all, it would create a group with a motivation to make—and responsibility for making—effective selections and placements on a "what's best for the whole government" basis.

There would be disadvantages, however. This plan would dilute the responsibility of agency heads, for choice of the people to run their programs is an essential part of their executive charge. Even though agency heads tend to retain the executives and professionals they have "inherited" (out of respect for their abilities, the need to depend on experienced executives, inertia, or the sheer difficulty of reassigning them), the right of choice is vital to their work. It may be argued in rejoinder that agency heads could be given a limited choice among candidates referred by the central staff. Their freedom of choice is limited by other circumstances now.

Another potential problem is that a central assignment process would be less sensitive to quality factors and special program needs in filling top jobs in the agencies. The central authorities might well be inclined to assign people who were "available" or "well qualified but not ideal," or who "need to be moved." This inclination would be reduced by their motivation to make high-quality placements, by the wide variety of jobs within which higher civil servants could be assigned, and by clearance with agency officials. Nevertheless, there will be many occasions when the need to place someone will be the paramount consideration.

Finally, the sheer magnitude of such a change would cause widespread controversy and insecurity in the higher civil service.[24] Employees would fear the effects on their freedom of choice and opportunity for progress. (As in any such change, their concern would probably be out of proportion to their actual difficulties.)

PRESIDENTIAL APPOINTMENTS TO HIGHER CIVIL SERVICE POSITIONS. Another alternative would be to establish a given number of top jobs (perhaps the present GS–18 managerial positions) to be filled by Presidential appointment, without Senate confirmation. Nominations could be made by agency heads, on recommendation of special selection boards. This plan would have the advantages of centrally controlled selection and would add special prestige to the process. It can be

[24] This was one of the factors that helped scuttle the Hoover Commission's Senior Civil Service plan.

criticized on grounds of (1) taking authority away from agency heads; (2) creating morale problems among higher civil servants not included; and (3) inviting political considerations to enter selections.

There are rejoinders to the criticisms: (1) agency heads would still have a major voice in selections; (2) somebody is always excluded from any group; and (3) politics has not dominated selections in other federal corps systems.

DECENTRALIZED SELECTION UNDER STRONGER CENTRAL CONTROLS. An intermediate alternative between the present pattern and any central assignment scheme would leave the appointing power with agency heads but impose stronger standards and controls over its use in order to assure greater breadth and more objectivity. Agency heads might be *required*, for example—

1. To establish formal selection boards operating under minimum prescribed procedures to recommend higher civil service selections.
2. To use systems of evaluating employees' potential that meet the seven "exacting requirements" suggested earlier in this chapter.
3. To inform the Civil Service Commission of vacancies in jobs in specified grades and in fields in which there is a probability that there are well-qualified candidates in other agencies; and to give evidence of formal systematic consideration of such candidates when they are referred.

Such requirements would have some tendency to delay selections, to result in some unproductive staff work, and to impair the morale of employees who expect to succeed to higher jobs. These are realistic disadvantages. It must be decided whether they are an appropriate or an excessive price to pay for increased objectivity and breadth of consideration.

Opportunity to Advance

The "chance to get ahead" was stated as a need to be met by a model personnel system. This is an oversimple concept, compounded of needs for money, status, and recognition. In the present study this element was measured and judged by upward progression in classification grades. (It is acknowledged that some federal executives and professionals do not aspire to the increased responsibility that goes with a higher grade. It is also acknowledged that there may be better ways of measuring progress, but most federal employees have never heard of them.)

Summary of Findings

WHAT ADVANCEMENT TOOK PLACE. The group studied did in fact advance significantly and steadily—an average of six to seven grades in 20 years (see Chapter 3). The Warner–Van Riper study (it included GS–14) reported an average time of 17.4 years for a career civil service executive to reach his present position. That study said that a "business leader" took 23.9 years to reach his present position, and a "military" executive, 25.4 years.[25] Another benchmark for comparison with military advancement is the statement by the "Bolte Committee" that "A schedule of promotion to . . . colonel/captain at 22 years would be . . . close to the statement of optimums by each service."[26]

Thus the civil service has provided, on the average, promotion opportunities that cannot be labeled unstatisfactory. It is difficult to determine whether the system provides adequate promotion opportunity to recognize fast-moving superior employees. A clear answer cannot be given, but is it noteworthy that 27 percent of the group studied reached their highest grade in less than 15 years of service, and 31 percent reached it under age 45.

EMPLOYEES' ATTITUDES ABOUT ADVANCEMENT. Members of the higher civil service covered by this study did not comment on rate of advancement as a leading source of either satisfaction or dissatisfaction.[27] They did suggest, however, that "more money" and "new opportunities" were reasons why others leave the service. It will also be recalled that 34 percent of the former employees who returned questionnaires left for "new opportunities," and 10 percent for "more money." Several of

[25] W. Lloyd Warner, Paul P. Van Riper, Norman H. Martin, and Orvis F. Collins, *The American Federal Executive* (Yale University Press, 1963), p. 384.

[26] *Report of the Department of Defense Ad Hoc Committee to Study and Revise the Officer Personnel Act of 1947* (December 1960), p. 29.

[27] In the *Image* study, federal executives rated the government above business on "chance to get ahead" and "chance to reach a top-level job." Kilpatrick *et al.*, *op. cit.*, p. 160.

the "outstanding" former employees interviewed said that they left the government because they could see no future beyond their "supergrade" positions. Perhaps some of them would have remained if they had been given more varied and interesting assignments. A further signal of discontent with the present situation is the frequently voiced dissatisfaction with regulations limiting the available number of "supergrade" positions.

Possible Courses of Action

PRESENT SITUATION. Advancement opportunities in the higher civil service are satisfactory on the whole, judging by the findings reviewed here. Despite the fact that the higher jobs may be filled from outside the government, there have been adequate chances for present employees to advance to them. Considering the higher civil servants' ages and intentions to retire (see Chapter 3), these opportunities will continue to be good, even if there is no expansion of government employment. This is, of course, a gross judgment. There are many individual situations in which superior employees who wish to and deserve to advance are unable to do so. They may already be in GS–18; or they may be blocked by unlikely-to-leave-soon superiors; or the "supergrade" quota may be full.

Opportunities in the higher civil service were improved in several respects by the Government Employees Salary Reform Act of 1964. For one thing, actual salary amounts for the top grades were sharply increased. Second, agency heads were given increased opportunity to make appointments above the minimum salary rates of GS–13 and above, subject to Civil Service Commission regulations. Third, the President was given authority to place some career positions in the lower "executive pay" levels provided by the Act: $27,000 and $26,000.

Despite these opportunities and improvements there will be cases in which superior employees are blocked from advancement. Hence some additional alternatives need to be examined.

FORCED ATTRITION. The military officer personnel systems force retirement of large numbers of officers in certain age and length-of-service groups to make room for the promotion of junior officers. The effect of such forced attrition is augmented by voluntary retirement of officers who are (or feel they may be) passed over for promotion.

The information on advancement opportunities presented in foregoing paragraphs strongly suggests that there is no need for a wholesale effort to open up more promotions. There may be cases where a mediocre official is "holding on," and an outstanding employee beneath him cannot be promoted. Such situations need to be handled by shifting or squeezing out the former (a subject discussed later in this chapter) by administrative action or involuntary retirement.

FURTHER "SUPERGRADE" FLEXIBILITY. Many of the advancement opportunities available in recent years have come through legislative liberalization of the quota limitations on "supergrade" positions. Limitations have been removed for scientific and engineering occupations, and more positions have been authorized for all categories. Limitations on the number of positions which the Civil Service Commission may place in the top grades increased from 550 to 2,400 from 1954 to 1964.[28]

Further liberality and flexibility in promoting superior employees to and within "supergrade" levels could be provided by several means:

1. Assigning quotas on "supergrade" positions to agencies and giving them freedom to place jobs in grades within these quotas without approval by the Civil Service Commission. This would make more rapid decisions possible. It would make agency heads responsible for maintaining proper alignment based on relative difficulty of the jobs. This liberalization would, however, invite the dangers of grade inflation and nonuniform administration.

2. Eliminating grade distinctions above grade GS–15. Employees would be paid salaries set by agencies within the GS–16 to 18 salary ranges. Agency heads would be guided by budgetary pressures and by considerations of internal equity in setting salaries. This change would recognize the difficulty of using job evaluation at these high levels of responsibility. It would also conform with the practice now followed for some scientific and engineering jobs. This approach would probably be criticized by Congress as not providing enough salary control.

SPECIAL TOP CAREER CATEGORIES. Another step to consider would be to establish special categories of jobs reserved for career employees in levels now occupied mainly by political executives. This would provide new top jobs to which higher civil servants could aspire and to which they could be appointed in recognition of truly superior merit. Partial precedents for such categories are found in the administrative

[28] *Actions to Improve the Higher Civil Service, op. cit.*, p. 8.

assistant secretaryships in several departments and in the career minister and career ambassador ranks of the Foreign Service.

Appointments to these categories could be made by the President without Senate confirmation [29] or (like the administrative assistant secretaries) by the agency head subject to Presidential approval. The group could be given some such designation as "Executive Corps" or "Presidential Corps."

A related idea might be considered: appointing properly qualified career employees as members of federal commissions or boards. This would not only have the benefits already suggested (targets for aspiration, tangible means of recognition) but would also put experienced employees at top decision-making levels. There would be a disadvantage: career employees would now be deeply involved in a political process, particularly if they became members of regulatory commissions. This would be a disadvantage, however, only if they were to return to managerial or professional duties. A commission membership could be the final federal job of a superior civil servant.

Movement To Meet Program Needs

A personnel system may be judged in part by the ease or difficulty with which changes of assignment may be made.

Summary of Findings

The regular "management" interviews in the present study showed some concern about this element. Although some 60 percent reported no difficulty in assigning personnel to meet program needs, the rest indicated a variety of obstacles. The "employee" interviews (where "employees" often made comments from a "management" point of view) showed significant support for means to increase ease of reassignment.

Chapter 3 reported a low degree of occupational mobility, inter-

[29] See discussion earlier in this chapter of possible Presidential appointments at the top of the civil service.

agency mobility, and headquarters-field mobility. This is not surprising, considering what it takes to move an employee to another job: management intent and staff machinery; incentives for the employee himself; the right combination of job duties and qualifications; and money.

Discussion with groups and individuals in the later stages of this study revealed a strong need for means of reassigning higher civil servants who are found to be poorly placed in their present jobs. The higher the grade level of such employees, the more difficult it is to find other jobs for them. Officials are also reluctant to exert pressure to displace such employees because they have civil service tenure in their jobs, and it is a prolonged, distasteful process to displace them through an adverse personnel action. This problem was one of the primary bases for the Hoover Commission's Senior Civil Service plan.[30]

Possible Courses of Action

PRESENT SITUATION. If nothing is done to change the present situation, agency heads will continue to have difficulty in making the personnel moves that they believe are necessary. Mobility in the higher civil service will continue to be low, and some less-than-acceptable employees in high jobs will assume the aspect of immovable objects. Management should be able to move them without "making a case" against them. This is particularly true in instances where a very able, respected employee should move because of policy differences with his superiors or because of previous close association with opposing political factions or abandoned programs. The freedom to choose and move top assistants is an important element in a political executive's control of his program.

CORPS, RATHER THAN JOB, AFFILIATION. Reassignment problems would be greatly eased if an employee's primary affiliation were not with a specific job, but with a corps, a cadre, a career. Then his rank and compensation would not depend on the job he holds, and neither his tenure nor his pay would be endangered by a move. The gains in

---

[30] Commission on Organization of the Executive Branch of the Government: Task Force on Personnel and Civil Service, *Report on Personnel and Civil Service* (Government Printing Office, 1955), pp. 56–58.

political control, management flexibility, and employee security would be clearly advantageous.

Whether the gains justify a change to a corps system is a difficult question. Such a change would mean a substantial abandonment of the job classification concept for higher civil service positions. It would also result in some change of present patterns of appointment authority. The power to place employees within the organizations to which they are being moved would have to be vested in persons other than the heads of those organizations. (The need for such a system is discussed in Chapter 7.)

INTERAGENCY PLACEMENT. Reassignments could also be facilitated with a more aggressive and effective central placement system. The Civil Service Commission should maintain complete and current qualifications records on all members of the higher civil service, along with information on types of assignments desired. (This would mean expanding the Career Executive Roster to include grade GS-15, a step being considered by the Commission.) This system will work well only if (1) it is staffed by able personnel specialists in sufficient numbers to have personal knowledge of the abilities and problems of the members of the roster (perhaps one to every 1,000 higher civil servants); (2) it is used and trusted by agency appointing officers; [31] and (3) adequate evaluative material on employees is available.

The principal arguments against a strengthened interagency placement system are: (1) that the government is doing well enough without it (an argument that can be made against any change); and (2) that the work required to maintain the system would be out of proportion to the benefits. The need for increased mobility as a means of development and for assurance that jobs are being filled by the ablest candidates suggests that such a strengthened system should be given a vigorous trial.

ELIMINATION OF JOB TENURE AT HIGHER CIVIL SERVICE LEVELS. Reassignments could be facilitated by another change: elimination of job-

---

[31] One frequently observed feature of the present system is personalized recruiting among officials' friends and acquaintances for vacancies not listed with the Civil Service Commission, and sometimes not listed with the agency personnel office. Conversations often end with the admonition, "Please don't tell anybody this job is vacant"—apparently because the speaker will not welcome unsolicited applications or referrals.

related tenure in higher civil service jobs. Many variations of such an idea can be devised, but the main idea is to permit employees to be taken out of higher civil service jobs without provisions for notice-and-reply, hearings, or appeals. They could retain tenure at the job levels previously held. Such a plan is now beginning to be installed in the California State Government, but it is too early to evaluate it. The California plan also features competition by examination for "Career Executive Assignments" with appointment under broadened certification rules.[32]

Such a plan recognizes the need for management flexibility in making higher-level reassignments. It may be defended partly on the ground that diminished security in the job is an appropriate price to pay for advancement to top levels. In any event, the employees would retain tenure in the civil service career system.

The plan can be opposed on the basis that a feeling of job security is necessary for good work performance and that abuses may arise through actions stemming from partisanship or favoritism. This objection could be overcome by providing for the Civil Service Commission to investigate complaints and report its findings to the agency head. His decision, however, would be final.

Another disadvantage is the indignity suffered by the employee who has to step down to his previous job level. This is a significant objection. The problem could be solved, or at least mitigated, by an effective placement system. It would be solved much more fully if a corps-affiliated, rather than a job-affiliated, system were in effect.

A variation of this plan that might be considered would be to make all appointments to "supergrade" positions for a stated number of years, perhaps three. Such appointments could be renewed.

Salary Levels

Summary of Findings

No salary surveys were made as part of the present study, but reference has been made to the staff work done by the Bureau of the

[32] California State Personnel Board, Personnel Management Bulletin No. 63–1, Nov. 4, 1963.

Budget, the White House, and the Civil Service Commission in connection with the Salary Reform Acts of 1962 and 1964. Congress has
approved the principle of making federal salaries comparable with
those in private industry and has raised the pay of the higher civil
service at the first step of the range by these amounts:

GRADE	BEFORE 1962 ACT	JANUARY 1964	1964 ACT
15	$13,730	$15,665	$16,460
16	15,255	16,000	18,935
17	16,530	18,000	21,445
18	18,500	20,000	24,500

Thus the 1964 Act salaries are increases of from 17 to 32 percent above
the pre-1962 levels.

The research in this study, done before the 1964 Act had made any
legislative progress, shows mixed reactions about salary. The management interviews yielded many comments that pay levels are not competitive with private industry and that this fact interferes with recruitment and retention of higher civil servants. Among the employees
themselves, pay was not a major cause of dissatisfaction. Both management and employees said that pay was the leading reason for leaving
federal service. It was found, however, that higher civil servants do *not*
leave the service in significant numbers for this reason. Management
and employees both favored higher salary levels and increased flexibility in setting rates.

Possible Courses of Action

PRESENT SITUATION. The 1964 Act, passed with the aid of strong administration backing, is based on a policy of seeking comparability with
private industry. By raising "executive pay" salaries, it became possible
to solve the many inequities resulting from the compression of salaries
around the $20,000 level. The government is not likely to achieve
complete comparability with the pay of top industrial executives, but
the levels in the 1964 Act are the highest ever paid to federal executives.

The current salary picture is still characterized by Civil Service
Commission control of some allocations to "supergrade" positions and
of qualifications of incumbents. This control is based on statutory

requirements enacted by Congress to prevent uncontrolled upgradings. Any such control is naturally distasteful to agency officials, who see it as a complicating and delaying factor. Unquestionably, it prevents some promotions that agency heads would like to make. The CSC controls doubtless result in more uniform and more conservative salary administration than would occur if they did not exist, but they do impair flexibility of management by agency officials.

DELEGATION OF CONTROLS TO AGENCIES. The difficulty of CSC controls would be solved in part by assigning quotas on "supergrade" positions to all agencies (some already have such quotas by statute) and by delegating to the agencies authority to allocate positions and approve qualifications. These changes would cut some red tape but would result in less uniform administration governmentwide. Agency heads would probably still contend that quotas were inadequate for their program purposes.

It would be possible to eliminate all quotas and trust to budgetary limitations to keep salary levels within reasonable bounds. It is doubtful if Congress would be willing to go this far. Such a change can be defended on the ground that the government has an obligation to pay its higher civil servants "what they are worth on the market," yet some agency heads would be sure to appraise the market more liberally than others and inequities would result.

Retention and Utilization

Summary of Findings

It has already been demonstrated that the higher civil service is a stable long-service group. Unlike the military officer personnel systems, the civil service system does not force out senior personnel who are making valuable contributions. In this study neither the management interviews nor employee interviews pointed to serious retention difficulties.

The Civil Service Commission does not maintain turnover data by grade levels, although this is now being started as part of the manpower forecast work mentioned earlier in this chapter. The author informally reviewed some of the preliminary figures and found that separation rates for the higher civil service grades are below 5 percent per year.[33]

Obviously such gross judgments leave much to be desired. The author learned of scores of superior employees, some of them with extremely scarce skills, who had left government service. One such loss may be more significant than the retention of a hundred other higher civil servants. This factor cannot be analyzed, however, without seeking quality judgments in depth.

There is more cause for concern about *future* turnover (see Chapter 3). Almost three-quarters of the present higher civil servants studied entered the service before 1946. Many of these are waiting for retirement eligibility.

With respect to utilization, the present situation seems favorable. The employees covered by this study spoke or wrote favorably of the challenge, interest, and importance of their work and said they were using their skills to advantage.

Possible Courses of Action

Retention and good utilization of higher civil servants would be affected by the possible alternatives that have been presented. These include more intensive training and development; more effective evaluation, selection, and placement devices; new advancement opportunities; or a corps personnel system. Superior executives and professionals would be longer retained and better used by any of such plans which remove artificial barriers to rapid development and effective placement.

NEED FOR A NEW LOOK AT RETIREMENT. Further study should be given to the rationale of the retirement system. A majority of the higher civil servants studied intend to retire long before their productive days are over. Retirement at 55 or 60 permits a man to start a new career. This can be looked at in two ways: (1) It is bad because the government could continue to use the employee's abilities. (2) It is good because the prospect of retirement is one factor that keeps the employee on the government payroll. It is doubtful if superannuation is really a factor in most cases.

---

[33] Said a knowledgeable but ungrammatical member of the Civil Service Commission staff, "They just ain't leaving."

It is reasonable to assume that the retirees want different work, or easier work, and want to maintain their present income levels. It follows, then, that the government might seek ways of placing these people in new work situations acceptable to them and pay them a suitable salary in addition to their annuities. Consider some theoretical examples:

1. An executive officer wants to retire at 55 and teach in a university. He could teach at Kings Point, or at the Industrial College of the Armed Forces, or at Annapolis.

2. A supervising auditor wants to retire at 58 to spend half of his time in accounting practice and half in hunting and fishing. He could be appointed to a half-time government accounting job in an area offering the recreational opportunities he wants.

3. A research and development chemist wants to retire at 60 to pursue some research and writing. He might be able to do this work in a government laboratory, working on a project helpful to the government.

In such cases the employees will have found interesting, satisfying work, and the government will have kept their skills. Such arrangements can be made under present law, but the employees cannot receive more *total* compensation (annuity plus salary) than the salary of the new job. This means that they have an incentive to seek non-federal jobs, where they can receive full salary plus full annuity.

Legislation could be considered to pay full salary, plus full annuity, in cases where the skills of a would-be-retiree would be of outstanding value to the government and could not be matched from any other source. Such legislation, to avoid abuses, would have to contain stringent criteria and would have to be very carefully administered, perhaps with all cases subject to approval by the Civil Service Commission.

Motivation

Summary of Findings

The great majority of the employees studied were well satisfied in general, interested in their work and working hard at it. One should note, however, the Kilpatrick finding that the federal natural scientists, social scientists, and engineers have slightly less positive attitudes about their occupational past, present, and future than their nongovernment counterparts have.[34]

Possible Courses of Action

To keep higher civil servants satisfied, or to make them even better satisfied, it is obviously necessary to maximize the factors that satisfy them and to minimize the causes of dissatisfaction. The former is a function of supervision and work assignments, for the main satisfactions of these employees relate to work challenge, accomplishment, pride in work, and sense of public service—factors that are inherent in the nature of their work.

It is difficult to reduce the causes of dissatisfaction. The principal "dissatisfier" was "government complexity"—factors like slow procedures, multiple clearances, excessive paperwork, too many rules, and duplication of effort. Such factors tend to be inevitable because of sheer organizational size, the defensive posture of government agencies, and the need for care and responsibility in carrying out public functions. They can be minimized, however, by resolute executive leadership and skilled management analysis studies.[35]

SPECIAL DESIGNATIONS OR CATEGORIES. Some of the higher civil servants indicated their desire for recognition as members of a special elite group within the government. There was no consensus on this factor, but it was brought up in various ways by people who took part in the study. Some deplored the disappearance of the old "P" service from the Classification Act in 1950, because they valued this formal "professional" label. Others urged the establishment of a special personnel system for scientists.

Since such special designations are lacking, the actual numbers of the GS "supergrades" have become symbols of aspiration and recognition. The statement, "He got his 16," is made with excitement which in other cultures might accompany bestowal of knighthood or a necklace of tiger's teeth. One of the reasons for considering establishment of

[34] Kilpatrick et al., op. cit., pp. 52 and 55.
[35] See also discussion of this point in Kilpatrick et al., op. cit., pp. 256–58.

one or more special corps in the higher civil service is this recognition factor.[36] It is also a reason for establishment of new high-level categories (discussed earlier in this chapter under "Special Top Career Categories"). The psychological need is to be a member of a group that is distinctive and difficult to join. This factor is one of the recognized values of other corps systems—the military officer groups, the Foreign Service, and the Commissioned Corps of the Public Health Service. It is one of the potential values really lacking in the civil service.

Some higher civil servants receive awards for distinctive work: the President's Award for Distinguished Federal Civilian Service, agency awards for distinguished or superior service, Rockefeller Public Service Awards, Career Service Awards (National Civil Service League), the Federal Women's Awards, and others. These awards can be given to only a small fraction of the higher civil servants, and they do not really meet the need for recognition as members of a larger—but still elite—group.

Creation of new group designations, however, would offer some problems. It would create new (and to some, unnecessary) distinctions to be made among people. Difficult decisions and bruised morale could be expected in determining which groups to include and which to exclude. Creation of new corps, ranks, or labels would also increase administrative complexities.

Mediocre or Unsatisfactory Personnel

Summary of Findings

The reassignment or dismissal of substandard employees is a perennial difficulty of all personnel systems. The judgments of management officials cited in this study were hard to interpret, but clearly pointed to some concern and difficulty in dealing with this problem. The officials interviewed did not on the whole consider it a major problem.[37] About three out of four reported success in dealing with substandard employees by various means, although some found these means (mainly

---

[36] Kilpatrick et al., op. cit., pp. 263–64.

[37] To some degree this response may be considered a defensive reaction. One cannot be sure without probing in much greater depth.

shifting or "shelving" employees) distasteful from both a management standpoint and a human relations standpoint. Said the deputy director of a large agency, "There are ways to do this, but they are expensive and they make us sick to our stomachs."

About one out of every four of the management group said that it was difficult or impossible to solve the problem. This view was shared by only about 5 percent of the employees who answered questionnaires. The remainder outlined a variety or succession of steps to deal with the problem.

Thus judgments on the seriousness of the problem differ, but it is clear that there are some very difficult and discouraging instances where higher civil servants are neither bad enough to fire nor good enough to keep—at least in their present jobs. They may be a negative, or at least inert, influence that slows program progress.

Shifting such people to other assignments is hindered by the inflexibilities discussed in this chapter under the heading. "Movement To Meet Program Needs." Getting them off the payroll is more difficult, if they do not want to go. Management officials are reluctant to take such action from a human relations standpoint. Formal dismissal procedures must be carefully planned and documented and are subject to appeal by the employee. Such actions are also distracting and upsetting to other employees.

Possible Courses of Action

PRESENT SITUATION. Leaving things "as is" would seem defensible in view of the careful concern for fair treatment that has been built into personnel procedures. The present situation is *not* satisfactory, however, if there are better means of helping management to get rid of mediocre or "slightly unsatisfactory" employees.

FIRMER EXECUTIVE LEADERSHIP. In discussing difficult cases, officials often referred to the need for more management fortitude.[38] This may suggest more top-level emphasis on the need for superior performance in the higher civil service. The President could stress that agency heads are *expected* to be rigorous in their requirements and resolute in dealing with those who do not meet them. Training and supple-

---

[38] Some said "guts."

mentary staff could be made available to operating officials who need assistance.

Such an effort would have some fairly obvious disadvantages. It would be labeled "purge" and would give the government a public-relations black eye. There is also the danger of erroneous actions due to partisanship or favoritism. These risks will have to be run if a decision is made that the situation calls for this sort of remedy.

MORE EFFECTIVE PLACEMENT. Strengthened interagency placement, which has already been emphasized, can be a means of shifting employees to jobs more suited to their capacities. This process must be managed carefully and responsively and not allowed to become a "lemon-passing" operation.

"SELECTION-OUT" BOARDS. The civil service system could establish boards of officials to review performance of employees and recommend reassignment or removal. Such boards (they have counterparts in military personnel systems and the Foreign Service) could be the same groups which consider selections for promotion (see the discussion under the heading "Selection," this chapter/ or could be different. Like the promotion boards, they should be representative of the organizations reviewed and should be made up of officials known for their mature and equitable judgment. The use of such boards would strengthen the fortitude of officials who know that action should be taken but are reluctant to initiate it. Their judgment would be shared, and action encouraged by the board.

Use of such boards will be most effective if they also work on "selection-up," or promotion, processes. Otherwise the selection-out board becomes a group of "hatchet men," whose very existence is a threat to morale.

SEVERANCE PAY. The separation of employees not yet eligible for retirement will be more acceptable both to them and to their associates if they are given severance pay to aid in their readjustment.

INVOLUNTARY RETIREMENT. Some management officials have said that the retirement system should contain a "two-way option"—that is, if employees have an option to retire early, management should have an option to retire them early. Thus the enactment of new provisions for involuntary retirement could offer a new means of getting rid of long-service employees who are coasting or who cannot adapt to the new needs of their agency programs. The legislation might provide that agency heads, subject to the approval of the Civil Service Commission, may effect involuntary retirement of employees over age 45 in grades 14 and above with more than 20 years service [39] whose performance and potential for future development are below the high standards expected for their grade levels. Such actions would be taken only after staff efforts to place the employee in a suitable position and after formal board action recommending retirement. This legislation would cover cases in which neither formal dismissal for cause ("the guy isn't that bad") nor reduction-in-force ("we still need the job") is appropriate.

The objections to this course of action are probably these: (1) It could be used for cases that, if handled with total honesty, *should* be dismissals or "RIF's." (2) It could be used to "railroad" good employees, although board consideration and Commission approval should prevent this. (3) It might be used, with connivance, for the benefit of employees who desire unjustifiably early retirement, but this too could be controlled. In general, the idea is attractive as offering one more avenue for action, and thus making personnel administration more flexible.

REMOVAL OR REDUCTION OF EXISTING PROTECTIONS. Another course worth considering is repeal or modification of some of the existing protections against adverse actions—notably Section 14 of the Veterans' Preference Act and Executive Order 10988, which extended veterans' appeal rights to nonveterans in 1962. These protections, plus a growing body of court decisions and implementing regulations, defend civil service employes from arbitrary, ill-considered dismissals. Indeed, with their legalistic, time-consuming complexities, they overdefend employees. Such provisions go far beyond the original notice-and-right-to-reply provision of the Lloyd-LaFollette Act of 1912. There has been a clear trend over the last fifty years to give civil servants more rather than less protection, and outright repeal or rescission of these measures would seem to have about as much political feasibility as painting the White House red.

[39] The reader may substitute other figures within any range he considers reasonable.

It might be considered more defensible to propose exemption of the top three or four grades of the civil service from these protections, so that agency heads would have a freer hand to assign officials best able to carry out their programs. As pointed out earlier in this chapter, the higher civil servants could be assured of career tenure in the last level held before they moved into the upper grades. The main arguments against eliminating tenure in the upper levels are that higher civil servants (1) have just as much right to retain their job level as "lower civil servants"; and (2) are likely to do more objective and responsible work if they feel secure in their jobs.

Conclusion

There are many feasible and attractive courses of action available to solve problems of the higher civil service. Choice among them will depend on the weight given the various factors summarized in the present chapter, the effect such choices have on the rest of the Civil Service, and budgetary and political considerations. In the following chapter the alternatives are grouped into four main patterns, and each pattern is evaluated.

7

Alternative Systems Compared

THE REMAINING TASK is to consider the best way to organize personnel administration for the higher civil service, in view of the specific evaluations presented in Chapter 6.

Criteria and Assumptions

The higher civil service personnel system should be such that it—

Maximizes factors that encourage improved quality, breadth, and flexibility of personnel

Minimizes factors that contribute to lessened quality

Maintains high, fairly uniform personnel standards throughout the government

Encourages best use of the government's executive and professional manpower resources

Does not conflict with assignments of responsibility for program results

Is acceptable to Congress, to agency heads, and to members of the higher civil service

Comes closest to meeting the criteria of a model personnel system (see Chapter 6)

Is adaptable to the variety of occupations, programs, and organizations in the federal service

It can be assumed that the following background conditions (summarized in Chapter 2) will continue to prevail:

A difficult and dynamic market for skilled manpower
A less-than-ideal image of Uncle Sam as an employer
A bureaucracy that grows no smaller, is resistant to change, and is governed largely by merit principles
Control of many details of personnel administration by Congress
A dominant role of agency heads in personnel administration

Possible Patterns Summarized

The *possible* variations in federal personnel systems are innumerable. Four main patterns have been selected for summary analysis here:

1. The present system, with due recognition of the way it is changing and developing.

2. The present system *plus* significantly more central leadership and servicing and extensive program innovations.

3. A governmentwide civilian corps system for the present top four grades of the civil service.

4. Corps systems for individual agencies.

In weighing the merits of these choices one must consider the degree of change in concepts and institutions called for by the present situation.[1] In other words, does the higher civil service need a new house, additional rooms for its present house, or only some new appliances in the kitchen?

1. The Present System as it is Developing

Data have been presented on the degree of satisfaction with the existing situation. The question is: "How much better can we do?"

The present system is dynamic and developing. The Civil Service Commission, for example, is establishing its manpower forecasting

[1] See discussion of "incremental change" and "calculated risk" in Paul T. David and Ross Pollock, *Executives for Government* (Brookings Institution, 1957), pp. 109–11.

scheme and has established the Executive Seminar Center. It is considering expansion of the Career Executive Roster and a number of other positive measures. Agencies have steadily strengthened their selection and development programs. Employee training activities have grown throughout the government. Staff specialists and committees work unceasingly to refine various aspects of the personnel system.

It is difficult to call the present developing situation unsatisfactory in view of the apparent quality of the higher civil service, and the attitudes of its employees and of agency management. If nothing new were done, the federal government would still have a reasonably good personnel system. Compared to most state and local governments, it is a superior system.

Nevertheless, as Chapter 6 has shown, the present system, even as it is developing, falls short of what a model personnel system ought to do in these respects:

1. Deep, detailed, qualitative analyses of future manpower needs at top levels.

2. Recruitment of superior new talent at intermediate and top levels (this will be needed less if the other objectives are met).

3. Provisions for interagency selection, placement, and development.

4. Long-term outside training for professional up-to-dateness and for perspective in public policy.

5. Opportunities to grow professionally and to advance in both pay and prestige above present "supergrade" levels.

6. Ease of reassignment of employees with career tenure.

7. Incentives to discourage premature retirement of superior executives and professionals.

8. Feasibility of shifting or dismissing mediocre or substandard personnel.

On a more general plane, the present system is handicapped by lack of consistent, well-focused leadership; the somewhat negative image of the Civil Service Commission among some agency officials; agency parochialism in personnel matters; the tendency to a personal, subjective *modus operandi* on the part of agency executives; and lack of incentives and opportunity for continued growth within the top grades of the service.

2. The Present System—Reinforced and Supplemented

The second major alternative pattern is a strengthened and refurbished version of the present system. The principles of the Civil Service Act and the Classification Act would continue to apply to the higher civil service; agency heads would retain appointing power; and the Civil Service Commission would keep its present responsibilities. In several important respects, however, the system would be new and different.

Executive Leadership

First and foremost, the Presidency would demonstrate and institutionalize far stronger leadership in personnel administration. The President would make it clear that he is deeply concerned with the necessity for superior personnel, particularly at the higher levels. From this point, two main courses are possible:

Plan A. The President would designate the Chairman of the Civil Service Commission as his representative in taking steps to improve federal personnel administration.[2] The Chairman already has executive authority to direct the programs of the Commission, but this would be strengthened by a clear indication of White House commitment and backing.

Plan B. A different approach would be the establishment of a staff within the Executive Office to act for the President in providing a central driving force to achieve progress. This office would not take away service or detailed inspection functions from the Civil Service Commission but would serve as leader, goad, and conscience. It would have to be headed by a person of recognized stature and superior executive ability. He would need able staff officers to assist him. Examples of their duties might include—

1. Meeting with agency heads to urge increased attention to higher civil service matters, to identify problems, and to exert continuing pressure for improvements in personnel programs, particularly in executive evaluation and development.

[2] As was done in the early years of the Eisenhower Administration.

2. Developing sources of recruitment for higher civil service personnel through contacts with industrial, professional, and educational institutions.

3. Developing means for assigning increased numbers of higher civil servants to outside educational programs.

4. Keeping pressure on agency personnel officers and the Civil Service Commission to maintain effective interagency placement and development programs.

5. Developing Presidential policies and programs to meet problems shared by the civil service, commissioned corps services, and other civilian personnel systems—for example, those of the Tennessee Valley Authority, the Atomic Energy Commission, the National Security Agency, and the Central Intelligence Agency.

6. Initiating studies of governmentwide problems, such as financing and personnel aspects of current federal retirement systems.

Such an office should not take over any personnel functions from the Commission but rather encourage strengthening of the Commission's central services on higher-level personnel matters.

Either plan could put more motive power behind strengthened recruitment, evaluation, selection, and development activities which are now inhibited by agencies' go-it-alone tendencies.

Plan A is organizationally neater. It gives both the President and the agency heads one channel, one principal source of advice, on personnel matters. It has the disadvantage of requiring the Commission Chairman to play different roles. As the principal merit system staff officer, he must at times limit, control, or even reverse actions by agency heads. They in turn may accept his leadership less fully than that of an official who has no regulatory or policing powers.

Plan B overcomes this disadvantage, but presents others: potential conflict, multiple channels, and possible slowdowns at top levels. There is also the danger that the Executive Office personnel staff might be assigned distracting or conflicting duties. On the other hand, such a staff could be so managed that it could add its strength to the Commission's and use the power of the Presidency to deal with obstacles that the Commission might find difficult. Since the Executive Office staff would not have operating or regulatory functions, it would be more free to "run with the ball" on new programs. The very establishment of such an office would have symbolic importance. It would be an institutional expression of the President's interest in the importance of the civil service, particularly the higher civil service.

Plan A should be tried first. It would be a smoother means of furthering new activities and of adapting them to what is already going on. If progress seems disappointing, Plan B should be put into effect.

With either arrangement, progress could be aided by another device: an unpaid commission of distinguished citizens who would study and report at suitable intervals on the government's higher civil service personnel system, both centrally and in its effects within selected agencies.

Other Innovations

With the aid of strengthened executive leadership, a number of the features discussed in Chapter 6 could be added to the present system:

1. A required agency-by-agency forecast-and-inventory system for higher personnel, tied in with the Civil Service Commission's forecast.

2. An aggressive recruiting program for middle- and higher-level executives and professionals of superior quality, to be placed in competition with present government employees. Some would be recruited for immediate consideration for higher civil service jobs; others for development programs leading to such jobs. In suitable instances, recruitment would be for short-term service rather than for career service. The Civil Service Commission would coordinate this recruiting, as it now does for college graduates, and would establish a new central recruitment office for this purpose.

3. Establishment and enforcement of more stringent standards for evaluation of employees considered for selection and development.

4. Compulsory, rigorous agency plans for development of employees for higher civil service jobs.

5. A drastic increase in long-term training assignments. (The present level of effort could be multiplied at least tenfold.)

6. Establishment of far more interagency and in-and-out-of-government developmental assignments.

7. Expansion of present executive seminars and other centrally sponsored training into a federal staff college.

8. Establishment of effective interagency selection and placement facilities (staff, records, and procedures), and required consideration of candidates from other agencies, at least for the three top grades.

9. Delegation of authority to agency heads to make classification and salary decisions within pre-set quotas for positions above GS-15.

10. Development of a plan to put a modest number of jobs in levels above the "supergrades."

11. Elimination of tenure-in-the-job above GS-15, with protection of the employee's previous salary and grade, at least temporarily.

12. Making an authoritative study of the benefits and disadvantages of a plan of employing annuitants on a pension-plus-salary arrangement.

13. Use of agency boards both to recommend selections for promotion and to identify and "select-out" mediocre and substandard employees in the top grades.

14. Addition of a new retirement category: involuntary retirement of persons in specified age, grade, and length-of-service categories whose performance and potential indicate that such action is desirable.

It should be obvious that these changes do not comprise an unbreakable package. Selections can be made from the list. Changes can be made at different times, as approvals and financing are obtained. The intent is to indicate a pattern of large-scale change without tearing up the present system completely.

Evaluation of This Pattern

These steps would greatly increase the government's effectiveness in getting, keeping, and using superior executives and professionals in top levels. Each step, although it may be criticized on various grounds, is in some way an improvement over present practice.

Some shortcomings of this pattern of changes are apparent:

1. No group or organization is given new or more effective motivation for the total improvement of the higher civil service. Agency heads, employees, and the Civil Service Commission may respond to stronger executive leadership, but their basic incentives would not be changed.

2. Costs of personnel administration would be increased, unless

they could be financed by forced economies in this or other fields of administration.

3. Some of these features can be regarded as a threat to present members of the higher civil service. Their advancement would be more competitive and their security in top jobs less assured.

4. The personnel authority of agency heads would be slightly curtailed, although with the purpose of having it used more effectively.

5. Salary administration would be less uniform and controlled.

This pattern offers changes that will solve many of the problems identified in this study and adopt some successful features from other personnel systems. It has dynamic qualities, yet retains the basic concepts of the present system.

3. A Higher Civil Service Corps

The creation of a centrally managed career corps for the higher civil service would be a more radical pattern of change.

Possible Features

Endless variations in detail are possible, but the following principal features of such a corps system will probably borrow enough elements from other corps systems to be an acceptable basis for discussion:

1. Limitation to prescribed levels. Here the present top four grades are postulated. Further limitations by arbitrary numbers or by specified occupations can be considered. It might be possible, for example, to establish one corps for scientists and engineers and another for other higher civil servants.

2. Competition for admission, in accordance with rigorous standards (although the initial cadre should be admitted on a "grandfather clause" basis [3]).

3. Rank and salary vested in the person rather than in the job assignment.

[3] Inclusion of all who satisfactorily occupy positions in the prescribed levels and occupations at the time the corps is established.

4. Centrally controlled assignment and promotion—probably by board procedures—including assignments to other agencies, to other geographic areas, and to educational institutions.

5. Planned individual career development, including both on- and off-the-job training and long- and short-term developmental assignments tailored to the individual's needs.

6. Selection-out of members with decreasing or marginal usefulness.

Evaluation of This Pattern

The main pros and cons of a governmentwide higher civil service corps are fairly clear from what has already been said in this report. To summarize the pros:

1. The corps would have great incentive value. It would provide a target for aspiration and a means of recognition.

2. Forecasting, inventory, and planning would be greatly facilitated because of centralized administration.

3. Reassignments would be more easily made, both for the employee's benefit and for management's. Tested executives and professionals could be assigned to new agencies or to incoming political executives. Career employees overidentified with previous regimes could be shifted.

4. Developmental programs to produce executives of breadth and versatility could be more easily managed.

5. Career orientation to the government as a whole would be encouraged.

6. Those administering the corps would have both the authority and the motivation to strengthen the higher civil service as a whole through selection, placement, development, outside education, discipline, and selection-out.

To summarize the cons:

1. The "elite group" aspect would be repugnant to many democratically minded citizens and employees and would suggest distasteful distinctions between members and nonmembers of the corps. (On the other hand, it must be recognized that corps status would be an earned distinction, based on competence.)

2. Many superior executives and professionals prefer to identify themselves with the program of an agency or bureau and would not care to serve with a governmentwide corps which could assign them elsewhere. Many would also oppose any reduction in the present high degree of individual initiative in making career changes.

3. The corps would tend to become a closed service, resistant to appointments above the entry level established. Its members might on occasion be motivated more by a desire to protect the corps than by more valid program considerations.

4. Central authority over assignment, promotion, and training of higher personnel would impair agency heads' control over their programs. Agency heads could be given power to approve or veto assignments, but such a provision would run counter to a basic reason for having a corps rather than the present system—namely, flexible central control of personnel.

5. The corps would have a tendency to encourage uniformity of attitudes, behavior, and even performance among its members rather than to develop personnel of diversity and flexibility.

6. Administrative complexity would be increased because of the need for special regulations, procedures, and records for administration of the corps.

DEGREE OF CHANGE FEASIBLE AND DESIRABLE. Establishment of a higher civil service corps would be a substantial change. Its installation would arouse excitement and controversy, judging by the history of the Senior Civil Service and Career Executive proposals. A change of this scope can be defended on the ground that the stimulus of newness is necessary to assure a higher civil service of continuing superiority. Such a change can be opposed by arguing that neither the findings of this study nor any other evidence call for more than incremental change.

Establishment of a corps *can* be regarded as one more step in a long series of improvements in the federal civil service. However, the concepts of authority and responsibilty in a corps system are very different from concepts in the present system. They will seem threatening to some employees and administrators; attractive and exciting to others.

4. Agency Corps Systems

This pattern would encourage agencies that look with favor on corps systems to establish them for their own professional and executive personnel.

Such corps systems would be most practical in bureaus and independent agencies of substantial size (say at least 3,000 employees), with field offices, and with a reasonably cohesive program or group of programs. They would have the features enumerated for the governmentwide system but would be limited to the personnel of the agency concerned and would, of course, be managed by that agency. Their establishment would be encouraged and approved by the Civil Service Commission and the President.

Within the civil service at present there are agencies that have many features of a corps system for their professionals and executives. These employees have identified themselves with the agency and its program; they rarely transfer to or from another agency; and they cooperate in career moves within the agency for their own development or to meet program situations. The Forest Service, the civilian staff of the Army Corps of Engineers, and the Food and Drug Administration are examples.

A possible (but difficult) variation would be to establish corps systems for groups of agencies whose missions and personnel needs are somewhat similar—for example, the Corps of Engineers and the Bureau of Reclamation, or perhaps the National Park Service, the Forest Service, and the Bureau of Reclamation. Many will be horrified by the idea of divided and cooperative personnel administration for organizations with such historic and sometimes bitter rivalries. Nevertheless, equally difficult problems of coordination have been solved at the Pentagon in recent years.

Evaluation of This Pattern

The establishment of agency corps systems would give more formal recognition and support to the tendency of employees to identify with particular programs and would increase their motivation and sense of security. It would give agency management more control and flexibility in managing transfer, development, and promotion programs. And it would permit the use of methods of evaluation, ranking, and compensation particularly adapted to the occupations and activities of the agency.

This change would have the disadvantage of discouraging personnel interchange with other parts of the government. The outlook of the agencies' staffs would tend to become or remain narrow, and opportunities to fill key jobs with superior personnel from other agencies would be reduced or eliminated. This alternative would also cause extra work and expense for each of the new systems in legislation, new regulations, procedures, controls, and so on.

Conclusions

The choice of one pattern—or of a combination of features from more than one—must be made with reference to some background factors:

The state of the manpower market for professional and managerial personnel.

The attitude of the Congress toward the President and its willingness to relinquish some of its participation in personnel policies and conditions.

The attitude of the public toward the federal service.

The attitudes of employee groups (both rank-and-file and professional)—a factor of ever increasing importance.

The degree of leadership that the President wishes to exert in the administration of the executive branch and the policies he wishes to follow.

The extent of satisfaction of all these parties with the present situation.

Choosing a course of action after assessment of these factors is a matter for decision by the President, on the advice of those with whom he shares the leadership of federal personnel administration—namely, the Chairman of the Civil Service Commission, the Director of the Bureau of the Budget, the Cabinet, and the heads of other agencies.

If the objective is merely to maintain the present level of achievement and progress, which is adequate in many respects, Pattern 1 should be chosen. This will be satisfactory to many representatives of higher federal management and probably to a majority of the present members of the higher civil service. Such a choice is defensible, although the strongest defenses come from those who have benefited from the system or who operate it. They are probably not aware enough of the shortcomings listed earlier in this chapter. They do not realize how much better the system could become.

If the objective is to rely primarily on present basic concepts of responsibility and yet move rapidly in making the higher civil service a more flexible and attractive instrument of national policy, Pattern 2 should be selected. New tangible evidence of Presidential leadership in personnel administration and a pattern of bold innovations will augment the ability of the federal personnel system to supply and keep top quality higher civil servants. Yet this pattern will be difficult to sustain. It calls for continued strong Presidential leadership; aggressive, positive work by the Civil Service Commission's Chairman and staff; and correspondingly strong leadership by agency heads and their personnel directors. Building and maintaining an excellent higher civil service is only one of their motivations—one which may be interfered with by other pressures.

If the objective of the leadership of the executive branch is to make the higher civil service a more cohesive, unitary, enduring *institution,* then Pattern 3 should be chosen. This pattern, as noted earlier, establishes a group whose primary motivation is to develop people for high-level service for the government as a whole. This is a factor which is missing from the other alternatives, and it may be a crucial one. The very newness of this course of action—the appeal of starting out in a new direction—is some assurance of success. On the other hand, its alteration of existing responsibilities and relationships will seem threatening to many, and the advantages could be submerged in resistance and controversy.

If the primary objective is to maintain strong, self-sufficient individual-agency higher civil service systems, Pattern 4 is to be chosen. This plan gives more formal recognition and prestige to professionals and managers in the various agencies but otherwise offers little advantage over the strong personnel programs of several agencies under the present system.

The choice of a course of action cannot rest on the assumption that the government is doing as well as it can in building a higher civil service. We can always do better.

Nor can the choice be based on the belief that there is an alarming need for reform. The shortcomings of the present situation are simply not that serious.

What is needed is strong, rapid, innovative action, demanded and led by the President, to make the higher civil service even better—action consisting initially of the steps listed under Pattern 2. Such action will bring significant progress beyond the present situation. This course involves stronger central leadership, reflected in requirements that agency heads must meet. There is no real threat, however, either to the authority of agency heads or to the status of truly able higher civil servants. Strengthened central requirements for forecasting needs, for recruiting, for evaluation of potential, for stepped-up development activities, and for use of promotion and selection-out boards will achieve progress in themselves. They will also be a step in the direction of establishing a governmentwide higher civil service corps. Experience will help determine whether it will be necessary or useful to go the rest of the way in that direction.

The higher federal civil service has done well in meeting the needs of these dynamic times. It can do better and it must do better, for federal programs are increasing in pace and complexity all the time. If the quality of the higher civil service is to keep up with the demands upon it, we cannot be content with the present rate of progress. The President, the agency heads, and the personnel executives must keep pushing, moving, developing, and innovating to improve this vital resource—this group of people whose work is so important to the nation.

APPENDIX A: *Survey and Sampling Methods*

Methods Used

1. *Review of Relevant Studies and Other Literature.* Library research was done by the project director and by Miss Frances M. Shattuck. Bibliographies prepared by the U. S. Civil Service Commission Library were very helpful. Abstracts of the federal personnel studies listed in the final section of Chapter 2 were prepared by Miss Shattuck.

2. *Management Interviews.* In all departments and major agencies, officials were interviewed to determine the effect of higher civil service personnel policies and problems on their organizations' programs. The project staff interviewed 100 officials [1] in the following categories:

Under Secretaries or Assistant Secretaries (and one Secretary) of Cabinet or military departments	12
Deputy Assistant Secretaries	5
Chiefs of independent agencies or of services or bureaus within departments	20
Deputy chiefs of agencies, services, or bureaus	6
Executive officers of agencies, services, or bureaus	5
Personnel directors of departments or agencies	14
Deputy personnel directors	2
White House staff members	3
Committee members or staff directors of related studies	7
Officials of the U. S. Civil Service Commission	16
Other	10
	100

A standard interview outline was followed, but interviewees were encouraged (little encouragement was needed) to express themselves freely. Interviewees were selected by the project director to cover a variety of agencies, professional disciplines, and hierarchical levels.

3. *Individual Employee Interviews.* Employees in the grades

---

[1] The total is actual, not artificially rounded.

studied were interviewed to determine how well their own career goals had been met in federal service.

As in the management interviews, an outline was used, but it was often followed loosely.[2] Of the 155 employees interviewed, 112 were selected by sampling.[3] The remainder were confidentially named by management officials as either outstanding or disappointing examples of higher federal employees. An effort was made to see if patterns of response for the latter groups were different from others. (There was, in fact, no discernible difference.)

The project interviewers sometimes had to exert control in interviews to keep "management" interviewees from responding as employees, and vice versa.

4. *Questionnaires to Present and Former Employees.* Questionnaires concerning career goals, job satisfactions, and personnel policies were sent to samples of present employees and of employees who had resigned or retired in recent years. One form ("PE") was used for present employees; a variant ("RE"), for former employees. Questionnaires sent and returned:

	PRESENT EMPLOYEES (Number)	FORMER EMPLOYEES (Number)
Questionnaires sent out	150	280
Undeliverable	13	46
Answered	103	98 [4]
Percent of response (deliverable forms)	*75%*	*42%*

Questionnaires were sent to present employees through their agency personnel offices; to former employees by mail at their last known addresses. One followup by mail was made in each case. All respondents were assured that replies would be treated confidentially.

5. *Statistical Analyses of Personal and Career Data.* Statistical analyses were made of personal and career data (age, length of service, occupation, agency location, education, mobility, and grade progression) for 363 present employees and 198 former employees. Personnel records clerks extracted the data from official personnel folders and entered them on "Career History Information Forms" designed for

[2] This outline and all other outlines and forms used in the study were pretested before use. Copies of all such documents are available in the project work papers.

[3] See the final section in this Appendix, "Sampling Procedure."

[4] Includes 15 responses from "former employees" who were actually present employees; these were tabulated as present employees. Also includes three questionnaires so incompletely answered that they were not tabulated.

this study. The completed forms were edited by the project director, then coded, punched, and tabulated by National Analysts, Inc. Coding and tabulating instructions were prepared by Brookings.

In addition to personal data about each employee, the following facts were recorded about his present position (or last federal position, in the case of former employees):

Title
Location: headquarters or field
Occupational series code
Grade
Department or agency
Bureau (or comparable organization)
Activity or installation

The same information was entered for positions held at five-year intervals: July 1, 1961; July 1, 1956; July 1, 1951; and so on back to the earliest such date on which the employee was employed by the federal government.

The "every five years" method was chosen primarily to minimize misunderstanding and error in obtaining career information. An alternative method, recording "last position," "position before last," and so on, would have been unreliable because of different interpretations of what a "position" is. The "every five years" method is accurate because it is so specific. It has the disadvantage, however, of incompleteness. The entries may not show the first federal position held. And they will not show instances in which there was more than one job shift within a five-year period. On the whole, however, the data obtained give reliable indications of career mobility and progression.

The dates chosen also show where employees were employed at strikingly different points in recent history:

Mid-Hoover Administration
Mid–New Deal
Early World War II
Post–World War II
Korean Conflict
Mid-Eisenhower Administration
"New Frontier"

6. *Group Employee Interviews.* Two luncheons were held at which four or five "supergrade" employees representing various disciplines and agencies discussed higher civil service personnel problems. At another luncheon five military officers, representing all three services,

discussed problems in their own personnel systems. Two dinner meetings gave a few federal officials and representatives of nonprofit organizations opportunities to discuss possible innovations in the federal personnel system. Another meeting was held with three of the principal officers of the Federal Professional Association. Finally, a meeting was held with a group of about 40 management interns to hear their views of higher federal positions and how to rise to them.

Final Analyses. Data produced by the foregoing methods were reviewed and summarized by the research assistants before final analysis and writing by the project director.

Sampling Procedure

Present Employees

The names of present employees who were interviewed or sent questionnaires, or who were the subjects of Career History Information Forms, were selected by sampling from two lists furnished by the Data Processing Center, Management Systems Division, U. S. Civil Service Commission. One was a 25 percent sample of the Commission's Career Executive Roster. It included employees of the Atomic Energy Commission and the Tennessee Valley Authority, as well as of the competitive service. The other was a 10 percent sample of employees in grade GS–15.

The project director determined that 475 "supergrades" and 375 GS–15's would be the population to be studied. This was a judgment based on the time, staff, and funds available. The number of "supergrade" names used is obviously disproportionate, as there are actually about five times as many GS–15's as "supergrades" in the federal service.[5] The proportion chosen gives a significant number of GS–15's, yet gives greater weight to employees in the top three grades because of the importance of their positions. It is therefore not claimed that the responses and other data in this report are statistically representative of all federal employees in the grades concerned.

The first list was reduced from 566 to the desired 475 names and

[5] As of June 30, 1963, Civil Service Commission figures showed 13,208 full-time employees in grade GS–15; 1,744 in GS–16; 696 in GS–17; and 313 in GS–18. (CSC *1963 Annual Report*, p. 32.)

the second from 1,364 to 375 by application of a table of random numbers. In the case of the second list, names of employees not on the General Schedule were skipped in this process.

Names were then selected from the reduced lists for interviews, questionnaires, and Career History Information Forms through application of this formula:

> Career History Information Forms: 1st, 3rd, 5th, 7th, etc.
> Questionnaires: 4th, 8th, 12th, 16th, 20th, etc.
> Interviews: 5th, 10th, 15th, 21st (to avoid subjecting the 20th to both interview and questionnaire), 25th, 30th, 35th, 41st, etc.

An effort was made to avoid selecting for interview or questionnaire employees who were being questioned in a concurrent study by Professor John J. Corson, of Princeton University.[6] When the formula of the present study would have selected a Corson subject, the next higher unused name on the list was taken instead.

The names selected for interviews and for career history data were augmented by those of 39 employees named by management officials as outstanding or disappointing examples of higher federal employees.

Former Employees

The former employees to be sent questionnaires were selected in two ways: (1) The Civil Service Commission supplied all the names on a list of former members of the Career Executive Roster; this totaled 145. (2) Sampling was used to select 135 names from lists of GS–15 employees who had resigned or retired from federal service in recent years; these lists were supplied by agency personnel offices.

These former employees are grouped as follows according to the years in which they left federal service:

DATE OF SEPARATION	(N = 196)
Fiscal Year 1963	22.6%
1962	47.7
1961	27.7
Earlier	2.0
	100.0

[6] The Corson study, tentatively titled *The Role of Top Level Civil Servants,* deals primarily with activities on which members of the higher civil service spend their time.

Career History Information Forms for former employees were prepared by the staff of the Federal Records Center at St. Louis from two lists: (1) names of former members of the Career Executive Roster; (2) names sampled from the lists of former GS–15 employees supplied by federal departments and agencies. Records were not found at St. Louis for many of the names supplied, so a supplementary list of former GS–15 employees (also sampled from the department and agency lists) was used until 200 forms had been prepared.

APPENDIX B: *Employees and Former Employees*[a]

Departments and Agencies	Number	Percent
DEPARTMENT OF DEFENSE		
Exclusive of military departments	29	5.2
Army	34	6.1
Navy	42	7.5
Air Force	47	8.4
OTHER CABINET DEPARTMENTS		
Agriculture	30	5.4
Commerce	50	8.9
Health, Education, and Welfare	28	5.0
Interior	21	3.7
Justice	13	2.3
Labor	16	2.9
Post Office	16	2.9
State	8	1.4
Treasury	10	1.8
AGENCIES		
Agency for International Development	2	0.4
Atomic Energy Commission	23	4.1
Bureau of the Budget	11	2.0
Civil Aeronautics Board	3	0.5
Civil Service Commission	7	1.2
Federal Aviation Agency	25	4.5
Federal Communications Commission	8	1.4
Federal Mediation and Conciliation Service	1	0.2
Federal Power Commission	3	0.5
Federal Trade Commission	5	0.9
General Accounting Office	4	0.7
General Services Administration	3	0.5
Government Printing Office	1	0.2
Housing and Home Finance Agency	11	2.0
National Aeronautics and Space Administration	54	9.7
National Labor Relations Board	4	0.7
National Science Foundation	1	0.2
Office of Emergency Planning	4	0.7
Railroad Retirement Board	1	0.2
Securities and Exchange Commission	1	0.2
Small Business Administration	4	0.7
Smithsonian Institution	2	0.4
Tariff Commission	4	0.7
Tennessee Valley Authority	7	1.2
Veterans Administration	19	3.4
Development Loan Fund	1	0.2
Export-Import Bank	1	0.2
U. S. Information Agency	4	0.7
District of Columbia Redevelopment Land Agency	1	0.2
Total	559	100.0

[a] For whom Career History Information Forms were tabulated.

APPENDIX C: *Major Occupational Fields of Employees and Former Employees*

Major Occupational Field of Present or Last Position	Total (N = 559)	Present Employees (N = 363)	Former Employees (N = 196)	Dept. of Defense (N = 152)	Other Cabinet Depts. (N = 192)	Other Agencies (N = 215)
Accounting	3.9%	2.2%	7.2%	5.9%	2.1%	4.2%
Aeronautics	3.2	3.0	3.6	2.0	—	7.0
Agriculture	3.6	4.1	2.6	—	8.9	1.4
Budget	2.7	2.8	2.6	2.6	1.6	3.7
Business or Industry	2.9	1.6	5.1	1.3	6.8	0.5
Economics	2.9	3.3	2.0	—	5.7	2.3
Education	1.1	0.8	1.5	—	3.1	—
Enforcement	1.6	1.4	2.0	2.6	2.1	0.5
Engineering	17.5	19.0	14.8	27.0	5.7	21.4
Finance—Credit or Loans	2.0	1.9	2.0	2.0	0.5	3.2
Insurance and Retirement	0.9	0.3	2.0	—	1.0	1.4
International Relations	0.9	1.1	0.5	1.3	1.0	0.5
Labor-Management Relations	0.7	0.8	0.5	—	—	1.8
Law	7.0	6.9	7.1	1.3	7.3	10.7
Manpower Resources	0.2	—	0.5	—	0.5	—
Medicine	1.4	0.6	3.1	—	2.6	1.4
Personnel	3.7	4.1	3.1	5.9	2.6	3.2
Physical Sciences, Mathematics, Statistics	13.0	15.4	8.7	25.7	7.3	9.3
Procurement	2.5	2.2	3.1	6.6	—	1.8
Public Information	0.9	0.6	1.5	1.3	0.5	0.9
Social Science and Welfare	0.7	0.3	1.5	—	1.6	0.5
Taxation	0.5	—	1.5	—	1.6	—
Transportation	0.9	0.8	1.0	0.7	2.1	—
General Administration	17.0	19.3	12.8	7.9	20.3	20.5
Management of Human, Financial, and Material Resources	4.3	4.1	4.6	2.6	8.3	1.8
Legislative Analysis	0.2	0.3	—	—	—	0.5
Architecture	0.2	—	0.5	—	—	0.5
Biology	1.1	0.8	1.5	1.3	1.6	0.5
Patents	2.0	1.7	2.6	0.7	5.2	—
Intelligence	0.3	0.3	0.5	1.3	—	—
Other	0.2	0.3	—	—	—	0.5

APPENDIX D: *Highest Level of Education of Employees and Former Employees*

Category	Present Employees (N = 362)	Former Employees (N = 193)	Total (N = 555)
High school	1.7%	2.6%	2.0%
Specialized school	1.1	3.1	1.8
Some college (not more than 2 years)	5.5	10.4	7.2
Some college (more than 2 years)	4.4	7.2	5.4
Bachelor's degree or equivalent	39.2	35.8	38.0
Some graduate work	14.1	8.8	12.2
Master's degree or equivalent	13.8	14.5	14.1
Some work above the Master's level	5.3	3.6	4.7
Doctorate or equivalent (including M.D.)	14.9	14.0	14.6
	100.0	100.0	100.0

Index*

Administration of federal personnel: changes needed in, 72–76; performed by career civil servants, 11; responsibility for, 12–16; suggestions for improving, 4. *See also* Agency heads; Civil Service Commission; Congress; President of the United States

Advancement of employees: average age and years of service in reaching top grade, 35–37; importance of, 8; number of grades advanced from first to highest, 37; opportunities for, 98–102; patterns of, 34–35; proposals for new job designations in achievement of, 101–2; rate of, 37–38

Agencies of the government: awards by for superior services, 111; employees' views on, 4, 63–64; personnel functions of, 14–15; planning by for future manpower needs, 79–80; possible action for training and development by, 93; present system of vs. corps system, 5; proposal for increased manpower forecasting by, 121; selection and development programs of, 118

Agency corps systems, 5, 126–27, 128. *See also* Corps system

Agency heads: in dealing with mediocre employees, 112–13; increased appointment authority of in salary Act of 1964, 100; need for leadership by in improving civil service, 129; possible increased authority for on classification and salary deci-

sions, 122; proposal for central control over personnel selection by, 98; responsibility of in personnel selection, 97; role of in administration, 16

Agency for International Development: personnel system of, 20, 51, 52

Alternative systems for the higher civil service, 5, 48–55, 116 ff.; choosing a course of action in, 127–29; four patterns selected for analysis, 117. *See also* Agency corps systems; Corps system; Military personnel system

American Assembly: report of on federal personnel, 16–17

American Federal Executive: a study on grades GS–14 and up, 20

Appeals on discharges, 15, 16

Army Corps of Engineers: features of corps system in, 126

Assignments to other jobs: as aid to career, 59; experience in state or local governments, 91–92; importance of for mediocre employees, 113; interagency use of, 5, 90–91, 104, 121. *See also* Mobility

Bolster, Mel H., 25n, 30n, 32n, 95n

Bolte, Charles L.: Bolte Committee statement on employee advancement, 99

Bureau of the Budget: filling top jobs in, 42; future manpower needs assessed by, 41; Office of Management and Organization in, 13; work of on salary levels, 105–6

Bureau of Employment Security (De-

* References to tables are in italics.

partment of Labor): forecasting of manpower needs by, 41

Bureau of Labor Statistics: future manpower needs assessed by, 41; study of scientists' mobility by, 32

Cabinet departments: personnel procedures in, 23, 35, 41, 42

California State: plan of for job tenure, 105

Career Executive Board: established by President Eisenhower, 13, 18; terminated (1959) by lack of congressional appropriation, 18

Career Executive Roster, 18, 23, 25, 30, 43, 95, 104, 118, 125

Career History Information Forms, 35, 37

Career Service Awards, 111

Careers in federal service: advice to young people on, 70–72, 71; helps and hindrances in, 58; satisfaction of high-level employees with, 59; stability of, 22

Categories of high-level jobs, proposals for: appointments to federal commissions, 102; establishment of one or more special corps, 111; separate designation for scientists, 110; special top career jobs, 101, 111

CED. See Committee for Economic Development

Characteristics of the group studied: classification grades of, 24; education of, 30–31; major occupational fields of, 24; percentages of employment by types of departments and agencies, 23; prior work of, 30; year of entry into service, 24. See also Former employees; Present employees

Civil Service Commission (CSC), 10n, 104n, 108n; actions of on employee career status, 58; Bureau of Inspections and Classifications Audits in, 42; Bureau of Programs and Standards in, 79; contrasted with corps system, 49; control of some allocations to "supergrade" positions,

106–7; created by Act of 1883, 12; functions of, 14–15; leadership of in salary reforms, 15, 106; number of top-grade positions authorized for placement by, 101; position registers maintained by, 43; program of in forecasting manpower needs, 42, 79–80, 117; proposal for maintenance of qualifications records by, 104; public information program of, 15; role of in personnel administration, 14–16; studies by on characteristics of career employees, 23; training stimulated by in Office of Career Development, 87, 88

Classification of jobs: Act of 1923, 12; Act of 1950, 110; advancement measured by, 98–99; employee views on, 74–75; improvements suggested for, 47–48; percentage of grades GS–15 to 18 in group studied, 24; rigidities in, 4, 42; role of agency head in, 16

Collins, Orvis F., 20n, 22, 25, 30, 99n

Commission on Organization of the Executive Branch of the Government, 17n, 73n, 103n. See also Hoover, President Herbert

Commissioned personnel system. See Public Health Service

Committee for Economic Development (CED): recommendations of on salaries, grades, and transfers, 21

Committee on Scientists and Engineers for Federal Government Programs, 19n

Competition of government with industry for key personnel, 9, 19, 50, 80–81; proposals for action on, 81–83

Conflict-of-interest rules, 42

Congress: committee attitudes toward federal employment, 12; in development of civil service programs, 5, 6, 8; legislation (1884) governing leave, 12; legislation to prevent uncontrolled salary upgradings, 107; principle of salary comparability approved by, 106; role of in personnel administration, 12

Cordiner, Ralph W.: report of "Cordiner Committee" on Department of Defense personnel, 19

Corps system: corps features presently exemplified in various agencies, 126; described, 49; flexibility of movement in, 54; high personnel motivation in, 111; ideas for government-wide corps system, 5, 123–25, 129; incentives for personnel development in, 94–95; meeting of program needs in, 53–54; motivation of employees in, 54–55; opportunity to advance in, 53; salary levels in, 54; selection of personnel in, 96. See also Alternative systems

Corson, John J., 22, 24n, 25, 27, 33

CSC. See Civil Service Commission

Cummings, Milton C., Jr., 1n, 10n, 14, 15n, 20, 21n, 59n, 79n

Curry, Robert B., 3n

David, Paul T., 18, 117n

Department of Defense: civil service employees in, 1, 23, 35; elite corps of scientists and engineers recommended for, 19; manning tables prepared by for training assignments, 90n; years of service and grades reached in, 36

Department heads: role of in administration, 16

Department of State: agency interchange of personnel recommended for, 52; selection-out practices in, 55; selection of specialized personnel in, 19

Development. See Training and development

Dismissals, 16, 48, 76, 114. See also Mediocre employees

Economic programs: need of high-caliber employees for, 6

Education of employees: level of, 30; variety of fields of study, 31

Eisenhower, President Dwight D.: ac-

tion of to improve the federal personnel administration, 119n; Career Executive Board established by, 18; fringe benefits sponsored by, 13; liaison office for personnel management in administration of, 13

Employees' views. See Former employees; Present employees

Engineers. See Scientists and engineers

Evaluation: of agency corps systems, 126–27; of employee performance and potential, 5, 50–51, 84–86, 121; of a higher civil service corps, 123–25; of the present civil service system, 117–18; of the present system reinforced and supplemented, 119–23

Examining and appointment procedures, 15, 81

"Executive Corps:" designation proposed for special top career categories, 101–2

Executive Seminar Center at Kings Point, New York, 87, 93, 118

Executives and professional employees: critical performance of in efficiency of government, 1; reasons of for leaving the service, 4; skill and knowledge of, 6; studies on, 19; training and development activities for, 44

FAME. See Federal Administrative Management Examination

Federal Administrative Management Examination (FAME): role of in qualifying applicants in field of administration, 81

Federal civil service: characteristics of, 11; size of and occupational variety offered, 10–11. See also Personnel system of the higher civil service

Federal Council on Science and Technology, 19

Federal Personnel Manual: evaluation requirements set forth in, 84; "merit promotion" plans presented in, 95

Federal staff college: plans for, 15, 92–93, 121

Federal Women's Awards, 111

Folsom, Marion: Folsom Committee Report, 20, 50, 52, 53, 79n

Food and Drug Administration: features of corps system in, 126

Forecasting needs. See Manpower

Foreign Affairs College: establishment of recommended, 52

Foreign Service: advance planning for manpower needs lacking in, 49–50; high personnel motivation in, 111; meeting of program needs in, 53–54; opportunity to advance in, 53; personnel system of, 2, 49, 51, 52; retention of personnel in, 54; selection methods of, 52, 53; studies by on specialized personnel, 19

Foreign Service Institute: success of in developing Foreign Service Officers through training assignments, 52

Forest Service: employment in at entry level, 11n; features of corps system in, 126

Former employees: age and length of service of, 28–29; ages on leaving the service, 29; reasons for leaving, 29, 99–100; responses of on comparison of federal and outside jobs, 69; views of on their careers, 4, 56 ff.

Fringe benefits: legislation on, 13; tendency of Congress toward, 12

General Schedule (GS): grade number a symbol of recognition, 110–11; levels of grades advanced, 35; other federal grading schedules, 35n; percentages of employees in GS–15 to 18, 24; total grades advanced, 37

Government contractors: professional leadership provided for by federal employees, 2, 6

Government Employees Salary Reform Act of 1964, 100

Group meetings for discussion of the civil service system, 9

GS. See General Schedule

Harris, Joseph P., 12n

Harrison, Evelyn, 23n

Hatch Act, 15

Health benefits laws, 12, 15

Herter, Christian A.: Herter Committee Report, 20, 50, 51, 52, 53, 54, 79n

Higher civil service employees: background facts about, 4, 22; critical performance of in domestic and international fields, 1, 5; dedication of, 42, 78n; dissatisfactions of, 61–63, 61, 77, 110; entry levels of, 11; GS grades of, 2n; industrialists' comments on, 3; motivation of, 109–11; number of executives and professionals in, 1; qualities needed in, 2, 6–7, 40; reasons for loss of, 45–46; retention and utilization of, 107–8; satisfactions of, 59–61, 61, 77, 110; sources from which obtained, 42–43; training and development activities for, 18, 44–45. See also Characteristics of the group studied; Present employees

Higher civil service personnel system. See Personnel system

Hoover, President Herbert: Hoover Commission on Organization of the Executive Branch of the Government, 17, 18, 73, 97n, 103

"Image" of federal employment: indifferent views on, 1

Image of the Federal Service: findings of on higher civil servants, 20–21. See also Kilpatrick

Industry: attracting specialists for federal service from, 10; federal experts' supervision of services performed by for the government, 2, 11

Insurance benefits legislation (1954), 12

Interviews: with employees, 9, 56 ff., 102; with management, 9, 39 ff., 81, 102, 106

Jennings, M. Kent, 1n, 10n, 14, 15n, 20, 21n, 59n, 79n

Job security, 60

Job tenure: effects of on work performance, 115; ideas on elimination of, 104–5, 122; problem of adverse action on, 103

Jobs in civil service: employees' initiative in decisions on placements, 11; how obtained, 56–57; problems in filling, 42–44; slowness of processing of, 42

Johnson, President Lyndon B.: salary comparability supported by, 13

Kennedy, President John F.: salary reform legislation enacted in administration of, 13; specialist in recruitment used by, 13

Kestnbaum, Meyer, 3n

Kilpatrick, Franklin P., viii, 1n, 10n, 14, 15n, 20, 21n, 59, 60n, 62, 79n, 82n, 91n, 99n, 110, 111n

Leaving the federal service: jobs offered outside the government, 57; reasons for, 29, 45, 66–68, 67, 106; and re-entering, 34, 67–68; sources of employee replacements, 69–70

Life insurance: administration of, 15

Lloyd-LaFollette Act (1912), 114

Management officials, views of: on attracting and keeping superior employees, 4; on changes desired, 47–48; on the higher civil service system, 39–48; on mobility, 102–3; on other federal personnel systems, 48–55

Manpower: advance planning for, 50; agencies, bureaus, and departments reporting plans for, 40–42, 79–80; forecasting needs and taking inventory, 40–42; market of the future, 9–10; needs of the future, 42, 49–50, 117; proposals for action on, 80; shortages in key occupations, 1, 9–10, 42

Martin, Norman H., 20n, 22, 25, 30, 99n

Masland, John W., 51n

Mediocre employees: means of dealing with, 5, 46–47, 55, 72, 111–15; overprotection of against adverse actions, 114–15; possible action in severance pay for, 113; rare occurrence of at top levels, 46; reluctance to take action against, 113; shifting of to other jobs, 8, 111, 113. See also Dismissals

"Merit promotion" plans, 95

Methodology of the present study. See Group meetings; Interviews; Questionnaires; Statistical analyses

Miles, Rufus E., Jr., viii, 73

Military personnel system: action of on future manpower needs, 50; different from regular civil service, 2, 48, 49n; emphasis of on professional development, 50–51; forced attrition of officers in, 100; high personnel motivation in, 111; meeting program needs in, 53–54; opportunity to advance in, 53; retention of personnel in, 54; selection boards of, 52

Mobility of employees: advantages of corps system for, 103–4, 105; departmental or agency moves, 33; effect of on continuous federal service, 34; geographical moves between field and headquarters, 34; increase in urged by management, 47–48; occupational moves, 31–33; percentages on workers' shifts to different organizations, 33; in program needs, 102–5. See also Assignments to other jobs

Moving expenses, problems of: in filling jobs, 42; in relocation, 75; in training assignments, 93–94

National Civil Service League, 111

Needs of the future for key personnel. See Manpower

Occupational fields in federal service, 1, 2, 6, 8, 9, 24n, 31n, 32n

Office of Executive Personnel in the

White House: proposal for creation of, 21

Performance and potential: proposals for improving rating system on, 76, 84–86. *See also* Evaluation

Personnel system of the higher civil service: assessment of and choice of a course of action for, 127–29; compared with other systems, 49; criteria for judging the effectiveness of, 6–8, 116–17; GS grades included in, 1, 2n; a pattern for a strengthened system, 119–23; quality and shortcomings in the developing present system, 117–18, 127–28, 129; substitution of a possible government-wide corps system for, 123–26. *See also* Alternative systems

Pincus, William, 17n

Political executives, 100–101, 103

Politics: freedom from in Hoover Commission plan, 17; "overtones" of in filling jobs, 42, 52; as reason for leaving federal service, 66; resentment of patronage, 11, 76

Pollock, Ross, 18, 117n

Present employees: age and length of service, 25–27, 27; eligibility of for retirement, 27, 28; judgments of on use of skills, 63; views of on civil service careers, 4, 56 ff., 78; views of on outside jobs, 68. *See also* Higher civil service employees

President of the United States: authority of in placing some career positions in "executive pay" levels, 100; need for innovative action by in personnel programs, 5, 8, 128, 129; proposal for appointments by to managerial positions, 97–98, 102; role of in personnel administration, 12–14; two plans for leadership by in a strengthened personnel system, 119–21

"Presidential Corps": designation proposed for special top career categories, 101–2

President's Award for Distinguished Federal Civilian Service, 111

Promotion: employee's initiative in arranging for, 11; merit programs for, 15; proposed means of liberalizing, 101; role of agency head in, 16; selection methods for, 53, 73–74, 122

Public Health Service: Commissioned Corps of, 49n, 50, 53; need of career development programs in, 52; personnel system of, 2, 20, 49; retention of personnel in, 54

Public Law 313, 22, 25, 75

Questionnaires completed by present and former employees, 9, 56, 58, 59, 72–73

Radway, Laurence I., 51n

Randall, Clarence B., 3n

Rank-in-job vs. rank-in-man principles, vii, 17, 47, 73

Recognition: importance of to employee, 8, 98, 110

Recruitment: activities in, 15; lack of central direction for, 81; need for improvement of, 5, 50; planning for by the CSC, 79; programs for in high schools and colleges, 10; proposals for action on, 4, 73, 82–83, 121; for vacancies not on CSC lists, 104n

Red tape, 4, 62, 66, 107

Reduction-in-force (RIF), 114

Reimer, Everett, 17n

Retirement: Act of 1920, 12; administration of, 15; involuntary category of, 113–14, 122; proposals for changes in, 76, 108–9, 122

Rockefeller Public Service Awards, 111

Roosevelt, President Franklin D.: civil service actions of, 12, 13

Salary: a cause of difficulty in filling jobs, 42; changes in desired by management, 47; employee dissatisfaction with, 62, 75; inflexibility of, 4, 5; levels of, 12, 105–6; possible action on achieving comparability of, 106–7; reform plans developed by the CSC, 15; Salary Reform Acts of 1962 and 1964, 9, 106

Sayre, Wallace S., viii, 12n, 13, 14n

Scientists and engineers: competition for, 9, 19; opportunities for, 8, 31n; a separate corps system suggested for, 123; years of service to reach highest grades, 36

Security checks, 15

Selection of employees, 16, 52–53, 73–74, 95–98; proposals for central controls of, 96–97; suggestion on interagency program for, 122

"Selection-out" system, 20, 55, 76; boards of officials suggested for, 113, 122

Senior Civil Service plan, 17, 73, 97n, 103, 125

Siciliano, Rocco C., viii, 13

Social programs: need of high-caliber employees for, 6, 10

Somers, Herman M., 17n

Staff college. See Federal staff college

Stanley, David T., 79n

State and local governments: services performed by for the U.S., 11

Statistical analyses on career data, 9

Staying in the federal service: reasons for, 64–65, 65

Substandard employees. See Mediocre employees

"Supergrade" employees: central placement roster of, 15; classification of, 16; federal staff college for, 92–93; selection of, 95–96

"Supergrade" positions: designation of, 18; filled by promotion, 95; GS number of as a symbol of recognition, 110–11; limitations on quotas of, 18, 19, 42, 75, 100, 101; proposal for levels above "supergrades," 122

Training and development: activities in, 15, 59, 86–89, 118; in alternative personnel systems, 51–52, 94–95; employees' initiative in, 11; ideas for action on, 75, 89–95; in-service and outside assignments in, 10, 45; legislation on (1958), 12; proposed compulsory agency plan for, 121

Transfer to another job: agency head's role in, 16; suggestions on, 73–74

Truman, President Harry S., 13n; classification amendments supported by, 12

Turnover in jobs: advance planning for manpower necessitated by, 80, 108; data on by the CSC, 107; lowness of in federal service, 42

United States Information Agency: personnel system of, 20, 51, 52

Van Riper, Paul P., 17n, 20n, 22, 23n, 25, 30, 33, 99

Veterans Administration: future manpower needs evaluated by, 41; personnel system of in Department of Medicine and Surgery, 49n

Veterans' Preference Acts, 12, 15, 114

Warner, Kenneth O., 3n

Warner, W. Lloyd, 20n, 22, 23n, 25, 30, 33, 99

White, Leonard D., 17n

Women: career patterns for, 23n; smallness of number of in the group studied, 23

Wriston, Henry: report of "Wriston Committee" on civil service and foreign service, 19

Young, Philip: influence of on federal personnel policies, 13; recommendations of "Philip Young Committee" (1957) on improving civil service programs, 19